/ 25

student power in world evangelism

inter-varsity press
downers grove
illinois 60515

david m. howard

Second printing, January 1971

*The Scripture quotations in this publication
are from the Revised Standard Version of the Bible,
© 1946 and 1952
by the Division of Christian Education
of the National Council of the Churches of Christ
in the U.S.A. and used by permission.*

*© 1970
by Inter-Varsity Christian Fellowship
of the United States of America*

*Inter-Varsity Press
is the book publishing division
of Inter-Varsity Christian Fellowship.*

*ISBN 0-87784-539-5
Library of Congress Catalog Card Number: 79-122918*

Printed in the United States of America

contents

preface

To state that we live in an age of rapid change is what a friend of mine calls "getting a strangle hold on the obvious." What could be more prosaic than to say that the world and all of society is in upheaval? Yet, prosaic or not, it is one of the overwhelming facts of our time that pervades all our life.

In the midst of this changing milieu, many are asking with increasing frequency, "Is the day of 'foreign missions' over? Is the missionary, as we have known him, an anachronism?" These are legitimate questions that must be asked. No realm of life is beyond the reevaluation of our rapidly changing society.

Few terms today turn off students faster than "foreign missions" and "missionary." The wierd and negative images which these words evoke, not to mention the violent opposition in many quarters, are widespread. This book is not a semantic treatise in defense of any specific words. If our changing times demand new words in place of those which no longer convey proper concepts, so let it be. Words in themselves are not sacred.

In the midst of revolutionary change all around us, one factor remains constant: the person of Jesus Christ who is "the same yesterday and today and forever." Akin to his unchanging character is the unchangeable task which he has given to his church.

It is the purpose of this book to examine that task from three perspectives: the biblical, the historical and the contemporary. Biblically, we will examine what God has to say about the responsibility of the church in the world. Historically, we will look at how students have responded to this task and what influence they have had on the world mission of the church. This study of history leads directly into an analysis of the contemporary scene. Mistakes of the past can be avoided today only if we understand what caused those mistakes. A rich heritage can only have value in giving us a richer future if we understand the principles which underlay that heritage.

With these perspectives in mind I hold firmly to the following convictions: First, Christian students will respond positively to Jesus Christ and his commands for world outreach when they see these in a biblical framework, free of the prejudices and cultural overtones of our times. Second, this student generation has a great heritage which it needs to understand. Third, the sovereign God of history will continue to call out a people for himself throughout the world. The present student generation has the exciting possibility of participating in this divine enterprise.

It is my prayer that this book will contribute in some small way to hasten that day when "the kingdom of the world has become the kingdom of our Lord and of his Christ."

—David M. Howard

PART I: THE BIBLICAL PERSPECTIVE

chapter 1

God—the originator of world mission

God's universal concern

Where does a discussion of the world outreach of the church begin? With the Great Commission—Go therefore and make disciples of all nations? With the book of Acts? With Pentecost? Hardly. The rapid spread of Christianity in the early church was, of course, the first major missionary thrust. But even it had a basis in the design for the world laid out and prepared for long before by God himself.

J. H. Bavinck, a Dutch theologian, has made the intriguing observation that "Genesis 1:1 is obviously the necessary basis of the great commission of Matthew 28:19-20."[1] "In the beginning God created the heavens and the earth." Here is where

---

[1] J. H. Bavinck, *An Introduction to the Science of Missions* (Grand Rapids: Baker Book House, 1960), p. 12. Johannes Blauw concurs: ". . . for an understanding of the universal purport of the Old Testament, it is necessary to have the Old Testament begin where it begins," *The Missionary Nature of the Church* (New York: McGraw-Hill, 1962), p. 17.

we must start to consider God's plan for his church and for the world. For it is in Genesis 1:1 that God immediately shows that the whole world is his concern.

God made the world; therefore he must have some interest in it. "The earth is the Lord's and the fulness thereof, the world and those who dwell therein" (Ps. 24:1). Having created the world, God fills it with the beauty of vegetation and animals, climaxing his handiwork by creating man in the image of God. This fact is at once the most profound and significant fact of the entire creation story. By making man in his own image God clearly and unequivocally shows his concern and interest in his created beings. He did not place man on earth simply to abandon him there. He created him capable of having fellowship with his Creator.

God's first command to man was, "Be fruitful and multiply and *fill the earth...*" (Gen. 1:28). Why fill the earth? God, having made the whole earth with all of its potential, desired to reveal his worldwide designs. "*Diffusion* unto the end of the earth was God's thought."[2]

But mankind rebelled against his Creator, willfully disobeying him and thus making fellowship impossible. Yet God, who is Love, would not have his purposes thwarted. He immediately began the process of redemption to bring man back into fellowship with himself. As early as Genesis 3:15, in the Garden of Eden, God gave his first promise of redemption which was to come through the woman's seed (Jesus Christ) who would conquer the serpent (Satan).

Man's rebellion, nevertheless, increased in intensity until the time came that "The Lord saw that the wickedness of man was great in the earth, and that every imagination of the

---

[2]Robert Hall Glover, *The Bible Basis of Missions* (Chicago: Moody Press, 1964), p. 15.

thoughts of his heart was only evil continually. . . . The earth was corrupt in God's sight, and the earth was filled with violence" (Gen. 6:5, 11). So God destroyed the earth by flood, saving only Noah and his family. When God then gave mankind a second chance, he repeated the command first given to Adam, "Be fruitful and multiply, and *fill the earth*" (Gen. 9:1).

Yet, strangely enough, this first of all commands given to man is the one he set about explicitly to thwart. This is highlighted at the Tower of Babel. God told man to move out to the ends of the earth. But man preferred to make a name for himself and feared the possibility of being diffused abroad. "Then they said, 'Come, let us build ourselves a city, and a tower with its top in the heavens, and let us make a name for ourselves, lest we be scattered abroad upon the face of the whole earth'" (Gen. 11:4). The purpose of the Tower of Babel was thus a self-centered one. It had two aspects. One was to make a name for mankind. The second was to provide a point of unity to prevent the scattering abroad across the whole earth.

When God saw that man, in his selfishness, was refusing to fulfill the first command given to him and repeated again after the flood, he intervened. In Genesis 11:5-9, there are four things mentioned that *the Lord* did, in contrast with what man had been doing (or failing to do). He came down, he spoke, he confused their language and he scattered them abroad. Thus the first outward movements of mankind across the face of the earth came as a result of divine intervention and not by human initiative. God had commanded this movement in the first place. Man had disregarded the command. So God intervened and forced compliance.

There is an interesting parallel to this in Acts. Christ had given his last command in Acts 1:8, outlining for the disciples the geographic progression which they were to follow in being witnesses. First Jerusalem, then Judea, then Samaria, then the end of the earth. The disciples diligently obeyed the command to witness in Jerusalem. But they somehow neglected Judea (the province in which Jerusalem was located), Samaria (the next province to the north) and the end of the earth. So once again God, having given a command that was being neglected, intervened and forced compliance. Acts 8:1 informs us that "a great persecution arose against the church in Jerusalem; and they were all scattered throughout the region of Judea and Samaria"—the very places Christ had told them to go to, but which they had neglected.

Again the purposes of God could not be thwarted. And fortunately the disciples got the point. From that time on, their efforts to extend the gospel were those of continuous outreach—"So that we may preach the gospel in lands beyond you. . . ." (2 Cor. 10:16). We are Christians today because the early disciples (once God forced the issue with them by means of persecution) were obedient in passing the gospel on to those beyond their own borders. Such divine interventions may even take place today. The author knows Christians in Colombia, South America, who first were pointed to Christ by refugees who had fled their home areas as a result of violent persecution.

God's purposes in israel
God Calls a Man. In order to carry out his purposes for the world, God begins with *one man.* Here he shows his pattern of working, repeated through the Scriptures and throughout the history of his people. God's basic method of working is through a man who will obey him and carry out his bidding on earth.

The story of the call of Abraham in Genesis 12:1-4 is a key

to understanding all the rest of Scripture and thus of God's plan for the world.

Now the Lord said to Abram, "Go from your country and your kindred and your father's house to the land that I will show you. And I will make of you a great nation, and I will bless you, and make your name great, so that you will be a blessing. I will bless those who bless you, and him who curses you I will curse; and by you all the families of the earth shall bless themselves." So Abram went, as the Lord had told him. . . .

This brief account contains a number of significant clues to God's plan of the ages. It is especially important to observe to what God was calling Abraham.

First, God did not call Abraham to a geographical location. There is no indication where Abraham is to go. He is simply told to get out of the land where he presently lived and to go to a land that God would show him. Why is this significant? Because it eliminates the possibility of confusing God's call with geography. To what, then, did God call Abraham? Eric Fife answers this when he says, "He was called primarily not to a country but to a Person. The key to his life is not his geographic location, but his relationship with God and obedience to His will."[3] Thus God's call was to God himself. When Abraham obeyed, in submission to God, he was then ready for further dealings from God.

Second, God's call was to mobility. The first word that God spoke to Abraham was "Go. . . ." Here he continues the theme laid down in the first command given in Genesis 1:28, repeated in Genesis 9:1 and forced upon man in Genesis 11 at Babel. God's people are to be mobile so that they may fill the

---

[3]Eric S. Fife, *Man's Peace, God's Glory* (Chicago: Inter-Varsity Press, 1961), p. 41.

whole earth. Harvey Cox makes some thought-provoking observations about mobility and its relationship to theology in *The Secular City*.

When we seek to understand the phenomenon of mobility from a theological perspective, it is well to remember that the whole Hebrew view of God arose in the social context of a nomadic, essentially homeless people. . . . In short, when they were wandering and homeless, the Hebrews seem to have been closest to fulfilling their calling. . . . The key characteristics of Yahweh, the Old Testament God, are linked to his mobility. He is the Lord of history and time. He is not spatially placed.[4]

Whether or not one agrees fully with its theological overtones, this statement highlights the fact that God is not bound to one place and will not let his people be bound to one place. The whole earth is his domain.

Third, God's call is to universality. "All the families of the earth" are to be blessed through Abraham. The obedience of one man becomes like the proverbial stone cast into the water of a pond, causing ripples that continue to reach out until the farthest shore of that pond is touched. Abraham, no doubt, could not understand fully the implications of this. We are permitted the hindsight of history and of the written Word of God, so we know what God refers to in this passage. Here he gives a promise that through the descendents of Abraham (the nation of Israel) would come the Redeemer, Jesus Christ. It is in Christ that all families of the earth are to be blessed. But while Abraham may not have seen all the facets of this promise, it was clear that God's purposes in him, as an individual man, had worldwide implications.

---

[4]Harvey Cox, *The Secular City* (New York: MacMillan Co., 1965), pp. 47-48.

This emphasis is repeated as God renews this promise to Abraham (Gen. 18:18; 22:17-18), to Isaac (Gen. 26:2-4) and to Jacob (Gen. 28:12-14). He never wants his people to forget that their calling is not parochial but universal.

God Calls a Nation. God, having started with one man and his family, now begins to build a great nation. This is the fulfillment of the promise, "And I will make of you a great nation" (Gen. 12:2). This nation will be a key human factor in God's redemptive purposes for the world. It has been chosen, not because it would necessarily be better than any other nation, but because it is to serve as the channel through which God's love to all nations can flow in the person of Jesus Christ. "The election of Israel is a matter of divine initiative which has as its goal the recognition of God by all nations over the whole world."[5] Thus Israel could never rightly conceive of itself as existing only for itself. The whole *raison d'etre* of Israel is bound inextricably with the worldwide purposes of God. "Israel had no reason to exist except as the bearer of an unmingled and undefiled faith in Jehovah."[6]

There are some unmistakable parallels between Israel of the Old Testament and the church of the New Testament. Just as Israel did not exist exclusively for its own interest, neither can the church exist for selfish reasons. It is an integral part of God's universal purposes of redemption, and the church must never be allowed to forget this.

God Calls the World. God, having called a man through whom he could form a nation, and having called that nation through whom he could reach the world, now extends his call to the world.

[Israel's] history was not a particular affair of no con-

---

[5] Blauw, p. 24.
[6] Bavinck, p. 18.

cern to anyone else, but . . . God utilized its history to deal with other nations, rather with the whole world. Israel's defeats and victories, its greatness and subjugations, its wonderful deliverances, and its heavy sufferings are all included in God's plan for the world. God stretches out his arms to all the world in such events.[7]

If he takes this one tribe to his heart for the time, it is not to forget the rest but to do good to all.[8]

Having laid the foundation for the fact that God's concern is the whole world (Gen. 1–11), then having formed a nation to reach that world, God now demonstrates this concern in the historical events surrounding his chosen people. Repeatedly through the Old Testament history of Israel, God did great things on behalf of them but with a greater purpose in mind. Many of God's miraculous performances had the immediate goal of delivering Israel; but they had the ultimate purpose of making God's name known among the nations of the world. A few examples will illustrate this.

When Israel was in slavery in Egypt, God produced ten plagues which finally forced Pharaoh to let them go. In the midst of this struggle God said to Pharaoh, "I will send all my plagues upon your heart, and upon your servants and your people, *that you may know that there is none like me in all the earth* . . . but for this purpose have I let you live, to show you my power, *so that my name may be declared throughout all the earth*" (Ex. 9:14, 16). Thus, while the immediate purpose of the plagues was to deliver Israel from Egypt, the broader purpose was to cause God's name to be declared through all the earth.

---

[7]*Ibid.*, p. 15.

[8]William O. Carver, *Missions in the Plan of the Ages* (Nashville: Broadman Press, 1951), p. 42.

As part of the exodus from Egypt, God performed two miracles of opening bodies of water. He opened the Red Sea so that Israel could march out of Egypt. Forty years later he opened the Jordan River so that Israel could march into the land of Canaan. Reflecting on these two great events Joshua said,

> For the Lord your God dried up the waters of the Jordan for you until you passed over, as the Lord your God did to the Red Sea, which he dried up for us until we passed over, *so that all the peoples of the earth may know that the hand of the Lord is mighty*; that you may fear the Lord your God forever. (Josh. 4:23-24)

It is remarkable that Joshua, who participated in both of these events and had led the Israelites into Canaan, had the insight to understand that God had an even greater purpose in mind in these miracles. It would have been easy for the immediate needs of Israel, which in both cases were very pressing, to have loomed before Joshua as the ultimate reasons for God's intervention. But he was able to see that God worked through Israel to make his name known throughout the earth.

One of the most familiar stories of the Old Testament is that of David and Goliath. The details of how God delivered Israel from the Philistines through the sling and stone of a shepherd boy need not be repeated here. What is not so familiar is how David, young as he was, perceived that God had a greater purpose than just the immediate deliverance of his people. David says to Goliath,

> This day the Lord will deliver you into my hand, and I will strike you down, and cut off your head; and I will give the dead bodies of the host of the Philistines this day to the birds of the air and to the wild beasts of the earth; *that all the earth may know that there is a God in Israel*. (1 Sam. 17:46)

David's son, Solomon, likewise perceived something of God's universal purposes when he built the temple in Jerusalem. At the dedication of the temple Solomon prayed at length, expressing his desires for the glory of God through the temple worship.

> Likewise when a foreigner, who is not of thy people Israel, comes from a far country for thy name's sake (for they shall hear of thy great name, and thy mighty hand, and of thy outstretched arm), when he comes and prays toward this house, hear thou in heaven thy dwelling place, and do according to all for which the foreigner calls to thee; *in order that all the peoples of the earth may know thy name and fear thee*. . . . Let these words of mine, wherewith I have made supplication before the Lord, be near to the Lord our God day and night, and may he maintain the cause of his servant, and the cause of his people Israel, as each day requires; *that all the peoples of the earth may know that the Lord is God*; there is no other. (1 Kings 8:41-43, 59-60)

The writers of the Psalms were also concerned that God's name should be declared throughout the earth. There are exhortations to worship for the whole earth: "Let all the earth fear the Lord, let all the inhabitants of the world stand in awe of him!" (Ps. 33:8). There are requests that God would act in such a way that his name would be known: "May God be gracious to us and bless us and make his face to shine upon us, that thy way may be known upon earth, thy saving power among all nations" (Ps. 67:1-2). There are calls to God's people to be active witnesses of their Lord throughout the earth: "O sing unto the Lord a new song; sing to the Lord all the earth! Sing to the Lord, bless his name; tell of his salvation from day to day. Declare his glory among the nations, his marvelous works among all the peoples! . . . Say among the nations, 'The Lord reigns!' " (Ps. 96:1-3, 10).

The prophets echo the concern of God's heart for the people of the whole earth to turn to him: "Turn to me and be saved, all the ends of the earth! For I am God, and there is no other" (Is. 45:22). There is even an occasional exhortation that Israel should aggressively announce to all the earth what God has done for them: "Go forth from Babylon, flee from Chaldea, declare this with a shout of joy, proclaim it, send it forth to the end of the earth; say, 'The Lord has redeemed his servant Jacob!' " (Is. 48:20).

It must be noted however that this is not quite the same as the missionary commands of the New Testament. In the Old Testament we find the necessary background for New Testament outreach, in which the church, under the commands of Christ, becomes responsible to carry his gospel to the ends of the earth. The Old Testament makes unmistakably clear that God's concern and his activity in history is on behalf of the entire world. "It is not the human activity that stands in the foreground of the Old Testament but the divine acts for the redemption of Israel. These acts cannot be confined to Israel, for the existence and redemption of Israel have consequences for the nations. The nations do not know this themselves, it has been avowed to Israel alone; but one day it will be avowed to the nations themselves." [9] And we might add that this avowing is to be done by the church.

Thus in the Old Testament God is at work in the world; in the New Testament God puts man to work to reach the world.

chapter 2

Christ—the foundation of world mission

the pattern of Christ's life

In the New Testament God individualizes his worldwide con·
cern showing that it is based on his love for each person. This
is dramatically stated in that profound yet wonderfully simple
statement, "And the Word became flesh and dwelt among us"
(Jn. 1:14). The Word—Jesus Christ, the Lord God—takes on an
individual human body and becomes a Man.

Boris Pasternak highlighted this in his masterpiece, *Doctor
Zhivago*. He compares the two great miracles of the Old and
New Testaments, the crossing of the Red Sea and the birth of
a child in a manger.

> What an enormously significant change! How did it
> come about that an individual human event, insignificant
> by ancient standards, was regarded as equal in signifi-
> cance to the migration of a whole people? . . . The reign
> of numbers was at an end. The duty imposed by armed
> force, to live unanimously as a people, as a whole nation,
> was abolished . . . replaced by the doctrine of individual-

ity and freedom. Individual human life became the life story of God and its contents filled the vast expanses of the universe.[1]

Using this as background, R. Kenneth Strachan shows how this emphasis on individuality, as exemplified in the Incarnation, becomes the pattern for mission for every disciple. Strachan illustrates how the Incarnate Son of God, as he walked through his earthly life, moved in three spheres of life and ministry.[2]

Relationship to His Father. Jesus, as an individual Man, recognized his need of fellowship with the Father. His private prayer life is graphically described throughout the gospels. Luke lays special emphasis on this, showing how Christ, before several of his major decisions or activities, spent time in prayer. Immediately prior to his temptation Christ prayed at his baptism (Lk. 3:21). Just before renewed opposition and a ministry of healing, he prayed (Lk. 5:16). Prior to choosing the twelve disciples he spent the entire night in prayer (Lk. 6:12). Just before Peter's great confession and the subsequent teaching concerning the cross, Christ prayed (Lk. 9:18). Before revealing his glory in the Transfiguration, he prayed (Lk. 9:28). Before teaching the disciples to pray, he prayed (Lk. 11:1). The night before his greatest crisis, he agonized in prayer at Gethesemane (Lk. 22:39-46). Finally, as he hung on the cross while his life ebbed away, he gave his final breath in prayer (Lk. 23:34, 46).

In Mark 1:35, we find Christ, after a particularly busy and exhausting day of teaching and healing, rising a great while

---

[1] Boris Pasternak, *Doctor Zhivago* (New York: Pantheon, 1958), p. 412.

[2] R. Kenneth Strachan, *The Inescapable Calling* (Grand Rapids: Eerdmans, 1968), pp. 50-57. For some parts of this discussion I am indebted to Strachan's exegesis.

before day and going out into a desert place alone to pray. Thus, Christ's own example speaks more eloquently than any words about the need of communion with the Father in prayer.

Relationship to His Disciples. Jesus chose his disciples prayerfully and with care. Yet he chose them from among the ordinary men of life, not from the religious leaders. They stand out primarily, not for their accomplishments nor their social or religious standing, but for what Strachan calls "their representative ordinariness." They were men of the common life, drawn from ordinary tasks, to become disciples. His purpose in choosing them was twofold, "to be with him, and to be sent out to preach" (Mk. 3:14).

First, they had "to be with him." They were to listen, watch, cooperate with him, help him.

He taught his disciples constantly, in the midst of the everyday situation in which they moved. It was on-the-job training; and as they experienced the joys and sorrows of serving the multitudes, of popularity and rejection, of success and failure, of the daily demands and constant fellowship with him, he molded and forged them into disciples.[3]

Next, they were "to be sent out to preach." Christ's whole purpose in making disciples was so that they, in turn, could carry out the ministry which he began on earth.

Christ's work of making disciples was carried out almost entirely in the midst of his ministry to the multitudes, and . . . it always had for its goal their eventual ministry to those same multitudes, thus bringing to realization God's ultimate purpose for them.[4]

---

[3] *Ibid.*, p. 56.
[4] *Ibid.*, p. 55.

Sometimes he taught them individually in personal conversation. (cf. Peter in Jn. 21:15-23). Sometimes he took a small group for special training (çf. Peter, James and John in Lk. 8:49-56; 9:28-36; Mk. 14:32-36). Other times he taught them as a group (cf. Mt. 13:10 ff). Often he taught them in company with the multitudes (cf. the Sermon on the Mount, Mt. 5–7).

He also used personal demonstration, letting them observe his methods of teaching, preaching and healing. He delegated responsibility to them, thus allowing them to participate in what was happening. In the Miracle of the Loaves he involved them by having them organize the people and then pass out the bread and fish (Jn. 6:1-14). He sent them out to preach and then to return to him for discussion of their experiences (Lk. 9:1-10; 10:1-20). He allowed them to fail so that they could see their own limitations and learn their dependence upon him; for example, when they were unable to heal an epileptic (Mt. 17:14-21).

Thus, when Christ returned to heaven, he was ready to say to them, "As my Father has sent me, even so I send you" (Jn. 20:21). He was entrusting to them the message of reconciliation (2 Cor. 5:19).

Relationship to the Multitudes. In his ministry to the individual and in training his handpicked core of disciples, Jesus was still very conscious of the masses of nameless people around him. "When he saw the crowds, he had compassion for them, because they were harassed and helpless, like sheep without a shepherd" (Mt. 9:36). "As he went ashore he saw a great throng; and he had compassion on them, and healed their sick" (Mt. 14:14). "Then Jesus called his disciples to him and said, 'I have compassion on the crowd, because they have been with me now three days, and have nothing to eat; and I am unwilling to send them away hungry, lest they faint on the way' " (Mt. 15:32).

To be sure, the reign of numbers was at an end. Each person was an individual whom Jesus Christ loved. But he also saw them as massive multitudes for whom he had compassion. Thus, in these three spheres of Jesus' life a pattern is laid down for his disciples and for all who subsequently follow him. The world mission of the church must be carried out on these levels: in fellowship with the Father, in the training of disciples who, in turn, can minister, and in compassion for the multitudes of the world.

the example of Christ's outreach

While his earthly ministry was primarily to the house of Israel and was confined to a relatively small area, Jesus nevertheless laid down certain principles of action by his example to his followers.

His Great Commission to evangelize the entire world was not given in full until after the resurrection. But early in his ministry Jesus showed by example that there must be a continuous effort to reach out.

Luke 4:42-43 relates how Jesus, after a very busy day in Capernaum withdrew to a lonely place, presumably for prayer and meditation. The people, however, sought him out, sensing that he was ready to move on. He had had a successful and satisfying ministry of healing and teaching in that area, and the people urged him to remain to continue this work. It is not hard to imagine the arguments they used.

"Consider how the people have been responding to your message. They are wide open. You must stay!"

"Look at how the sick and needy flocked to you yesterday. They were so pitiful in their infirmities and so wonderfully changed after you healed them. They will be your disciples for life."

"Think of all the other sick and demon-possessed that have not yet had contact with you. You must remain and heal them as well."

"Look at all the corruption and poverty that remains in Capernaum. This city is far from evangelized yet. You must remain until we get the job done here. Why move out to preach in some other town until your preaching has cleaned up the mess right here?"

Perhaps some went so far as to suggest that his moving elsewhere was "escapism," that he was merely trying to avoid the problems of Capernaum.

All of these arguments sound legitimate and logical. Yet what was Jesus' answer? It was short and to the point, yet it had far-reaching significance for the mission of the church he was to found. He simply said, "I must preach the good news of the kingdom of God to the other cities also; for I was sent for this purpose." He did not deny the crying needs of Capernaum. He did not argue that he had finished the job there. He did not pretend that all the evils of that city had been corrected, that there was no more injustice or poverty there or that there were no needy people who could benefit by his physical and spiritual healing. Rather he directed their attention to the fact that the "other cities also" were in need of help. The worldwide concern of God so clearly expounded in the Old Testament becomes the same concern for God's Son. He cannot neglect the others who have not yet heard his message.

This is the same principle enunciated in his discourse on the Good Shepherd. After describing the sheep, the shepherd and their relationship to each other, he says, "And I have other sheep, that are not of this fold; I must bring them also, and they will heed my voice. So there shall be one flock, one shepherd" (Jn. 10:16).

When the early church began its mission, it had not only the commands of Christ telling them to go into all the world. It also had his own example of continuous outreach to others who had not yet heard the good news which he brought. The principle of mobility implicit in the call of Abraham is now exemplified by the Son of God.

the commands of Christ for world mission

Jesus Christ was not a non-directive leader. That is, he did not just set an example (although he clearly did that) and then expect his disciples to draw their own conclusions. Rather, he expressed in unmistakable declarations and imperatives his plan for them. No single statement of his will for his church is more clearly enunciated in definitive directives than that which has come to be known as the Great Commission. An understanding of the full import of the gospel is impossible without an understanding of this commission.

There are five passages in the New Testament where this commission is given. It is important to notice the time and place of each, as well as to analyze the particular emphasis given on each occasion.

The first passage, chronologically, is found in Luke 24:33-49. This is the story of what took place on the evening of the resurrection day. The disciples had gathered together behind closed doors and were discussing in bewilderment the events of the past three days. Suddenly Jesus appeared in their midst. This is the first time that Jesus had met with his disciples as a group since before the crucifixion. What could he be expected to say to them on such an occasion?

No doubt they remembered that the last time they had been with him as a group, at the hour of his greatest crisis when the soldiers came to arrest him, ". . . all the disciples forsook him and fled" (Mt. 26:56). Now in their fear and perplexity, it is quite possible that they fully expected to be rebuked for their cowardly behavior. However, Jesus completely ignored the past when he began to speak.

First, he allayed their fears and doubts by proving that he was really alive. "Why are you troubled, and why do questions rise in your hearts? See my hands and my feet, that it is I myself; handle me, and see; for a spirit has not flesh and bones as you see that I have" (Lk. 24:38-39).

Then he turned their attention to the Old Testament Scriptures about himself. "Everything written about me in the law of Moses and the prophets and the psalms must be fulfilled. Then he opened their minds to understand the scriptures" (Lk. 24:44-45). Next, he gave a brief summary of the gospel, "that the Christ should suffer and on the third day rise from the dead."

At this point he made a significant connection: he summarized the gospel and immediately made the following thought germane to it—"and that repentance and forgiveness of sins should be preached in his name to all nations, beginning from Jerusalem" (Lk. 24:47). That is, the preaching of the good news to all nations is a necessary part of the gospel, for without this the message has no way of becoming effective in the lives of men. His next statement is one of commission. "You are witnesses of these things" (Lk. 24:48).

Jesus knew that the first thing he said to his disciples following the resurrection would doubtless make a great impression on them and would probably remain in their minds longer than many other things he said. So he chose the most important thing he had left to get across to them, namely, that they were now responsible for the extension of the good news of salvation to all nations.

In John 20, the same incident is recorded. However, John's wording of Jesus' commission to the disciples is different from

Luke's. Jesus said, "As the Father has sent me, even so I send you" (Jn. 20:21).

There are two possibilities for the difference in the two accounts. One is that Luke and John simply use different words to record the same idea expressed by Jesus. Another possibility is that Jesus expressed the same idea twice during the evening, using different words each time in order to get his point across. This is a good principle of pedagogy. Given the fact that no two words in the commission are alike in Luke and John, this second alternative seems to be the most likely. Jesus seems to have wanted his disciples to be sure to catch the implications of what he was saying, so he repeated it in two different ways the same night.

Matthew gives the most complete expression of the Great Commission found in the gospels: "And Jesus came and said to them, 'All authority in heaven and on earth has been given to me. Go therefore and make disciples of all nations, baptizing them in the name of the Father and of the Son and of the Holy Spirit, teaching them to observe all that I have commanded you; and lo, I am with you always, to the close of the age' " (Mt. 28:18-20).

It is significant to note where this was given. Verse 16 informs us that this took place on a mountain in Galilee. Hence it cannot be the same incident Luke and John record taking place in Jerusalem on the day of Christ's resurrection. Jesus was thus repeating his commission at another time and place, indicating its urgency.

It is also important to observe that the only imperative verb form in the passage in Matthew is the verb "make disciples." The word "go" in the original is in the participle form. It could be translated, "As you go, make disciples of all nations." Jesus apparently was assuming now that they would go. He had already told them that they were to be his witnesses to all nations (Luke 24) and that he was sending them (John 20). Now, assuming that they would go, he tells them that the essence of their work is to make disciples. This means to bring men into a relationship to Jesus Christ so that they can be baptized and follow him by observing all that he had taught them. This process of discipling becomes the key to the work of spreading the gospel which Jesus commends to his followers. They are not just to scatter the seed in an indiscriminate manner. They are to cultivate men in such a way that they become true followers of Jesus Christ.

Mark gives us the shortest and most frequently quoted of the Great Commission passages. "Go into the whole world and preach the gospel to the whole creation" (Mk. 16:15). The time and place of this occasion are not made clear. Mark simply says, "Afterward he appeared to the eleven themselves as they sat at table" (Mk. 16:14). No indication is given as to whether this is the evening of the resurrection day (as recorded by Luke and John) or the occasion in Galilee on a mountain (as recorded by Matthew). Possibly this could even be a third occasion at some other time and place.

But the most significant fact about Mark's account is that he did include this in the gospel story. [5] With its inclusion in Mark's gospel, the Great Commission appears in all four gospel accounts.

This in itself is no small point. Very few events or teachings in the life of Jesus appear in all four gospels. For example, a story as beautiful and as important as the Nativity appears in

---

[5] Mark 16:9-20. (I am well aware of the critical problems surrounding the text of Mark 16:9-20 and of the fact that its inclusion in the gospel is disputed. However, I am accepting the position of numerous scholars who believe that the textual evidence is sufficient to accept this as an authentic part of the gospel narrative.)

only two out of the four. Only one of the numerous miracles he performed is recorded in all four (the Feeding of the Five Thousand). But when we come to the death and resurrection of Christ, all four writers must include these, for without them there is no gospel ("good news"). Likewise, without the Great Commission (the commending of the good news of salvation to the disciples for the purpose of taking this news around the world) the gospel story is incomplete. Unless the news of the death and resurrection of Jesus Christ becomes known to mankind, it is of no value to him. Consequently, all four gospel writers must record this commission as an integral part of the narrative.

In Acts 1, we find the account of Christ's ascension to heaven. He had risen from the grave and appeared to his disciples over a period of forty days. Now the time had come to return to his Father. He gathered them together on the Mount of Olives for final instructions. When they began to question him about the timing of God's kingdom, he replied, "It is not for you to know times or seasons which the Father has fixed by his own authority. But you shall receive power when the Holy Spirit has come upon you; and you shall be my witnesses in Jerusalem and in all Judea and Samaria and to the end of the earth" (Acts 1:7-8).

This is a complete yet concise outline of the mission which Christ gave to his church. *Who* is to do the job? "You. . . ." *What* will be given to make this job possible? "You shall receive power. . . ." *When* will this take place? ". . . When the Holy Spirit has come upon you." *Why* is this power given? ". . . You shall be my witnesses. . . ." *Where* is the witnessing to be done? ". . . In Jerusalem and in all Judea and Samaria and to the end of the earth."

Note the geographical pattern developed here. They were to start where they were—in Jerusalem. Then they were to continue throughout the province (Judea) where Jerusalem was located. Then they were to push out to the next province, Samaria. But they were not to stop until they reached "the end of the earth." The universality of God's plan for the world, emphasized to Adam, to Noah, to Abraham and to their descendents, once again becomes evident as Jesus Christ outlines his plan for the mission of the church.

The timing of this declaration is also profoundly important. We read, "And when he had said this, as they were looking on, he was lifted up, and a cloud took him out of their sight" (Acts 1:9). Thus, the words spoken in verse 8 were the last words that Jesus Christ ever spoke on earth. Jesus knew human psychology. He knew that the last words spoken by a loved one will be remembered. Consequently he chose the words which at this point were the most important—the commission for them to carry the gospel to the end of the earth. It is quite probable that they returned to Jerusalem with these words ringing over and over in their ears, "You shall be my witnesses . . . to the end of the earth . . . to the end of the earth . . . to the end of the earth." How could they ever forget these final words spoken by the Master whom they had come to love and to serve?

We know Jesus Christ today because those early disciples were not disobedient to the final command which Christ gave to them.

chapter 3

the holy spirit—the power for world mission

the holy spirit's relationship to the great commission

In our study of the Great Commission one extremely important element was purposely left for consideration at this point. It is this: In every one of the passages where the commission is given, some reference, either direct or indirect, is made to the Holy Spirit.

Matthew 28:19 refers to "baptizing them in the name of the Father and of the Son and of the Holy Spirit." Mark records the promise that "these signs will accompany those who believe. . ." (Mk. 16:17). He then proceeds to list certain signs which will accompany the preaching of the gospel. These signs are either gifts or direct actions of the Holy Spirit through the believers. Luke records that as soon as he had given the commission, Jesus added, "And behold, I send the promise of my Father upon you; but stay in the city, until you are clothed with power from on high" (Lk. 24:49). This refers to the promise of the coming of the Comforter (cf. Jn. 14:26; 15:26; 16:13-14), and the empowering that would take place at Pentecost. John, having stated the commission, adds, "And when he had said this, he breathed on them, and said to them, 'Receive the Holy Spirit' " (Jn. 20:22). Acts 1:8 gives the statement of Jesus, "But you shall receive power when the Holy Spirit has come upon you; and you shall be my witnesses. . . ."

In this context, and referring to the witness of the early church, Harry Boer makes the startling statement that ". . . there is no evidence that consciousness of the Great Commission constituted an element in their motivation."[1] This may sound like heresy, especially since we have just been emphasizing the importance that Jesus himself placed on that commission. However, Boer goes on to clarify this by stating,

> . . . The Great Commission played a powerful role in the missionary witness of the early Church from the day of Pentecost to the present. It can be said that it always has been, is now, and always will be the heart and soul of all true missionary witness. But its meaning for and place in the life of the missionary community must, we believe, be differently construed than is customarily done. The Great Commission . . . derives its meaning and power wholly and exclusively from the Pentecost event.[2]

> We do not wish to suggest that the command of Christ was not at all in the mind of the early Church. So far as we know, however, it formed no part of her motivation. And that is significant. It indicates that in the judgement of God the ideal form of witness is that which takes place through inner compulsion. Witness began not with

---

[1] Harry R. Boer, *Pentecost and Missions* (Grand Rapids: Eerdmans, 1961), p. 43.

[2] *Ibid.*, p. 47.

the receiving of the Great Commission, but with its *internal effectuation* at Pentecost. . . . Pentecost made the Church a *witnessing* Church.[3]

Boer thus highlights the fact that without the coming of the Holy Spirit and his influence upon the lives of the apostles and other believers, the commands of Jesus Christ for world evangelism never could have been carried out. The Holy Spirit is the power which makes possible the worldwide outreach of the church.

the holy spirit's relationship to the church in outreach

When the Holy Spirit was given to the church on the day of Pentecost (Acts 2), he began his work in the lives of all believers. Every person who receives Jesus Christ into his life thereby receives the Holy Spirit: "Any one who does not have the Spirit of Christ does not belong to him" (Rom. 8:9). As the Holy Spirit works in each life, part of his work is on behalf of God's plan for the church to extend itself around the world. He does this in various ways.

The Holy Spirit Fills Men for Power in Witness. In Acts there are nine occasions when either a group or an individual was filled with the Holy Spirit. It is significant to note how this filling affected the people involved and the people who looked on.

On the day of Pentecost, when the Holy Spirit came initially upon the church, "they were all filled with the Holy Spirit and began to speak in other tongues, as the Spirit gave them utterance" (Acts 2:4). The immediate result of the filling was that they spoke "the mighty works of God" (Acts 2:11) so that all the travelers in Jerusalem on that day could hear the message in their own languages. And the ultimate result was

---

[3] *Ibid.*, pp. 128-129.

that three thousand people repented of their sins and were baptized (Acts 2:41).

It was not long before the preaching of the gospel evoked opposition from the religious leaders of the day. Peter and John were summoned before the authorities and questioned severely about their preaching. Peter, filled with the Holy Spirit (Acts 4:8), answered boldly and clearly, giving the essential gospel message. Thus, the effect of the fulness of the Spirit in Peter was boldness to proclaim the gospel. The result for others was that "all men praised God for what had happened" (Acts 4:21).

Later the same day, when Peter and John reported to the other Christians, they all joined together in prayer, asking for courage to witness. Immediately "they were all filled with the Holy Spirit and spoke the word of God with boldness" (Acts 4:31). The result was a sense of unity and great power among the apostles and believers (Acts 4:32-33).

Shortly after this the apostles came under criticism for neglect of the widows among them. So they appointed deacons who could serve the material needs of the church, while the apostles gave themselves "to prayer and to the ministry of the word" (Acts 6:4). These men were required to be "of good repute, full of the Spirit and of wisdom" (Acts 6:3). When Spirit-filled men were chosen and began their duties on behalf of the church (duties which were primarily of a material nature), the result was that "the word of God increased; and the number of the disciples multiplied greatly in Jerusalem, and a great many of the priests were obedient to the faith" (Acts 6:7).

Stephen was one of these deacons chosen to serve the needy in the church. In the course of his activities and preaching, he also came under severe criticism from the religious leaders. Called before the high priest, he delivered a brilliant sermon showing how Jesus of Nazareth was the fulfillment of all the Old Testament developments through the nation of Israel. The message so pricked the consciences of his listeners that they began to stone him. At that moment he was filled again with the Holy Spirit (Acts 7:55), was given a vision of heaven and prayed with his dying breath, "Lord, do not hold this sin against them" (Acts 7:60). This prayer requesting forgiveness for his murderers so impressed a young man standing nearby that he later became a follower of Jesus Christ. Thus, the fulness of the Spirit in the life and death of Stephen became a vital link in the conversion of Saul of Tarsus, better known as Paul the Apostle.

When Saul was converted, he, too, was filled with the Holy Spirit (Acts 9:17), and "in the synagogues immediately he proclaimed Jesus, saying, 'He is the Son of God' " (Acts 9:20). Again the result was the conversion of many others. Acts 9:25 refers to *"his* disciples," indicating that these were people who now followed Christ as a result of Saul's teaching.

As the rapidly spreading gospel message began to take root in other cities, the apostles in Jerusalem felt a responsibility to help newer believers. So they sent Barnabas, "a good man, full of the Holy Spirit and of faith" (Acts 11:24), to help the young church in Antioch. The fulness of the Spirit gave Barnabas wisdom in leading these new Christians in their faith and the result was that "a large company was added to the Lord" (Acts 11:24). Antioch soon became so vital a church that it seemed to replace Jerusalem as the center of growth and outreach. It was at Antioch that the disciples were first called "Christians" (Acts 11:26). It was from Antioch that the first missionaries, Paul and Barnabas, were sent out to carry the gospel message to other areas (Acts 13:1-4).

On this first missionary journey Paul and Barnabas soon met satanic opposition through a sorcerer named Elymas on the island of Cyprus. A defense was needed against the subtleties of Satan, and it came when the Holy Spirit filled Paul and gave him the courage and power to rebuke the sorcerer in no uncertain terms: "You son of the devil, you enemy of all righteousness, full of all deceit and villainy, will you not stop making crooked the straight paths of the Lord?" (Acts 13:10). This was hardly the type of language calculated to win friends and influence people, but it was promoted by the fulness of the Spirit in Paul to deal with opposition to the message of salvation. Elymas was struck with blindness for a time. When the proconsul, who had been a close friend of Elymas, saw what had happened, he believed in the Lord (Acts 13:12).

Later, on the same journey, the disciples at Iconium "were filled with joy and with the Holy Spirit" (Acts 13:52). The result of this filling was that they "so spoke that a great company believed, both of Jews and of Greeks" (Acts 14:1).

In every one of these cases two elements were present. First, when the disciples were filled with the Holy Spirit, they inevitably said or did something for the furtherance of the gospel. Second, the result was that some people believed.

Thus, the fulness of the Holy Spirit is necessary for effective witness and should result in that witness.

The Holy Spirit Gives Gifts to the Church for Outreach. In addition to filling believers so that they can witness effectively, the Holy Spirit gives special gifts to the church. The full teaching about gifts is found in Romans 12, 1 Corinthians 12 and Ephesians 4. Several factors need to be noted in order to understand their place in the church.

First, these gifts are a result of the grace of God and are not earned by man: "Having gifts that differ according to the grace given to us . . ." (Rom. 12:6). Second, the gifts are given through the Holy Spirit: "All these [gifts] are inspired by one and the same Spirit who apportions to each one individually as he wills" (1 Cor. 12:11). Third, gifts are given to all believers in one form or other: "To each is given the manifestation of the Spirit . . ." (1 Cor. 12:7). Fourth, the purpose of the gifts is "for the common good" (1 Cor. 12:7). That is, they are to be used on behalf of the entire church. This is emphasized also in Ephesians 4:11-12, "And his gifts were . . . for the equipment of the saints, for the work of the ministry, for building up the body of Christ. . . ."

A list of twenty spiritual gifts can be culled from the three chapters mentioned above (wisdom, knowledge, faith, healing, miracles, prophesy, discernment, tongues, interpretation of tongues, apostles, teachers, helpers, administrators, service, exhorters, contributors, giving aid, acts of mercy, evangelists and pastors). It is probable that Paul was not attempting to give an exhaustive list in any of the epistles. Rather, he was giving examples of some of the gifts which God gives to his people to edify them personally so that they, in turn, can serve to build up the body of Christ. Some of the gifts mentioned are probably identical with others called by a different name in another epistle. But the important thing to note is that the Spirit of God equips his people to carry out his work.[4]

The Holy Spirit Chooses Some for Special Outreach. In Acts 13:2, the Spirit said to the church at Antioch as they were worshipping together, "Set apart for me Barnabas and Saul for the work to which I have called them." Every believer is to be a witness, but some were selected for a particular outreach. Notice that this choosing came at the initiative of the Holy Spirit and not from men. It also came through the church and in the context of worship. It was not an isolated

---

[4] For a fuller discussion of the gifts of the Spirit, the danger of excesses in seeking or using these gifts, and how to keep the biblical perspective, see Appendix I.

choice of two individuals but rather a recognition of their relationship to the church, the body of Christ. These men were then sent forth by the church, commended and supported by their fellow believers who had recognized the special call of the Holy Spirit.

The Holy Spirit Guides Men in Outreach. Throughout the story of the expansion of the early church, as recorded in Acts, the Holy Spirit demonstrates how he can guide his people. Sometimes he would lead a disciple *to one individual*. This was the case with Philip in Acts 8. Philip had been having an effective public ministry to masses of people in Samaria. But the Spirit told him to leave Samaria and go down into the desert. Not knowing what awaited him there, Philip obeyed. There he met the Ethiopian eunuch, whom he pointed to Jesus Christ and baptized. The eunuch "went on his way rejoicing" (Acts 8:39), carrying his newfound faith to his fellow countrymen in a far-off land.

Sometimes the Spirit led a disciple *to an ethnic group*. In Acts 10, God spoke to Peter through a vision to prepare him to do something he would not otherwise have done—to go into the home of a Gentile. At the same time he spoke to Cornelius (the Gentile) to tell him to send for Peter. When the invitation came to Peter, the Spirit told him to go to the home of Cornelius without hesitation. Peter obeyed, and he became God's instrument to open the door of faith to the Gentiles.

At times the Spirit led *to a specific geographical location*. In Acts 16:6-9, there is a series of significant geographical references. Paul and Silas, on the second missionary journey, had preached the gospel in eastern Asia Minor. Then they tried to go south but were "forbidden by the Holy Spirit to speak the word in Asia." Turning north they headed for Bithynia, "but the Spirit of Jesus did not allow them." Thus the leading of the Spirit at times could be negative by not allowing one to go in a given direction.

Having preached in the east, and having been hindered from going either north or south, they headed west. Arriving in Troas, a seaport, they had gone as far as they could. At this point the Spirit gave them a vision of a man of Macedonia inviting them to come over and help. Paul and Silas obeyed, thus taking the gospel into Europe for the first time. This was clearly the result of geographical leading.

the holy spirit's relationship to the world

As the church, under the power of the Holy Spirit, obeys Jesus Christ in outreach to the world, the Spirit carries on his work also in those to whom the message is being given. When Jesus promised the coming of the Spirit (whom he called on this occasion "the Counselor"), he said, "And when he comes, he will convince the world of sin and of righteousness and of judgment; of sin, because they do not believe in me; of righteousness, because I go to the Father, and you will see me no more; of judgment, because the ruler of this world is judged" (Jn. 16:8-10).

It is the work of the Holy Spirit to convict men of their sin and of coming judgment. No human witness, however eloquent or persuasive, has the power to cause conviction in the heart of an unbeliever. Conviction is the work of the Spirit of God. Likewise it is his work to draw men to Jesus Christ in repentance.

Thus, while God was the originator of world mission and Jesus Christ the foundation of world mission, it is the Holy Spirit who is the power for world mission.

chapter 4

the church—the agent of world mission

the church and mission

The Apostle Paul says, "God was in Christ reconciling the world to himself . . . and entrusting to us the message of reconciliation" (2 Cor. 5:19). That is, God has completed the work of reconciliation in the death and resurrection of Jesus Christ. But the task of sharing this message has been entrusted to those who have been reconciled—namely, the church.

Peter reinforces Paul's statement when he speaks of the church and says, "But you are a chosen race, a royal priesthood, a holy nation, God's own people, that you may declare the wonderful deeds of him who called you out of darkness into his marvelous light" (1 Pet. 2:9). One purpose of God's calling his people is that they may declare his wonderful deeds. Blauw highlights this when he says, "A 'theology of mission' cannot be other than a 'theology of the Church' as the people of God called *out* of the world, placed *in* the world, and sent *to* the world." [1] He elaborates this further by saying, "There is no other Church than the Church *sent* into the world."[2]

If the church is not reaching out into the world, it is failing in the very purpose which God himself declares is basic to the existence of the church. D. T. Niles of Ceylon states, "Missions must cease to be a specialty, and be seen instead as an integral part of churchly obedience." [3] Bishop Lesslie Newbigin adds, "Missions are not an extra; they are the acid test of whether or not the Church believes the gospel."[4]

The church has been called *out* of the world to be a holy people for worship and fellowship with God. God has placed the church back *in* the world to serve as light *to* the world. Jesus said, "As long as I am in the world, I am the light of the world" (Jn. 9:5). But he stayed in the world in bodily form only a short time. So he also said to his disciples, "You are the light of the world" (Mt. 5:14). Since he is no longer here in person, it is up to the church to keep the light of his gospel shining in the world. The church is responsible to see that this light penetrates into the farthest corners of the earth. If there are places where the light still has not penetrated (and there are), the church must examine itself to find out why.

Any self-examination by the church (by each individual in the church as well as the corporate body) should include a study of the apostolic church. The characteristics and strategy of the early church, which was so eminently successful in penetrating the whole known world with the gospel in a short

---

[1] Blauw, p. 126.

[2] *Ibid.*, p. 121.

[3] D. T. Niles, *Upon the Earth* (New York: McGraw-Hill Book Co., 1962), p. 10.

[4] Lesslie Newbigin, *Is Christ Divided?* (Grand Rapids: Eerdmans, 1961), p. 32.

time, should be helpful in evaluating our responsibilities today.

characteristics of the early church

The book of Acts serves as a basis for understanding the church of the first century. The epistles also give insights into the problems and strengths of the church. What are some of the characteristics which emerge from a study of Acts and the epistles?

Obedience. From the beginning the church was obedient to God and to the commands of Jesus Christ. We noted in Chapter 1 that at one point God had to force this obedience through persecution that scattered the believers abroad. But once that initial hurdle was passed, there is every evidence that the church continued in a constant effort to obey the last command of Christ.

Before the scattering by persecution Peter preached in *Jerusalem* on the day of Pentecost and three thousand people came to Christ (Acts 2). Peter and John healed a lame man at the temple and then explained the gospel to those who questioned (Acts 3–4). Stephen preached to the Jewish leaders (Acts 7).

Following the persecutions Philip went to *Samaria* and preached to great multitudes (Acts 8). From there he went to the desert road and testified to the Ethiopian eunuch (Acts 8). Ananias in *Damascus* spoke to Saul of Tarsus (Acts 9). Peter went to the household of Cornelius and shared the gospel with the Gentiles for the first time (Acts 10). Barnabas went to *Antioch* to help build up the new believers there (Acts 11). And Paul and Barnabas were sent out from Antioch on the first of three great missionary journeys (Acts 13), the story of the rest of Acts.

Sensitivity to the Holy Spirit. Acts abounds in references to the Holy Spirit, who is mentioned more than fifty times. We have already noted in Chapter 3 that the Spirit filled the believers for witness, guided them into outreach and endowed them with gifts for implementing Christ's commands.

One of the keys to the growth of the early church was their sensitivity in responding to the promptings of the Spirit. When the Spirit told Philip to leave a thriving revival in Samaria and go out into the desert, he went. When the Spirit told Peter to go to the household of a Gentile, he went. When the Spirit told Ananias to go to speak with Saul of Tarsus, the great persecutor of the Christians, he went. In each of these cases the individual's preference would have been not to do what he was told. But in each case his obedience resulted in a furtherance of the gospel.

Prayer. The early church was a praying church. They prayed for guidance and it was given (Acts 1:24-25). They prayed in worship (Acts 2:42). They prayed for courage to witness (Acts 4:24-30) and "the place in which they were gathered together was shaken; and they were all filled with the Holy Spirit and spoke the word of God with boldness" (Acts 4:31). The answer was immediate.

They prayed for each other when someone was commended to a special task (Acts 6:6; 13:3; 14:23). They prayed for power to perform miracles, and the dead were raised (Acts 9:40). They prayed for Peter's deliverance from prison (Acts 12:12) and an angel of the Lord came and removed Peter's chains, opened the prison doors at night, and set him free while they were still praying. Here they were quite human in their praying. When Peter appeared at the door of the home in which they were gathered, they could scarcely believe that Peter was free.

Paul and Silas prayed in prison (Acts 16:25) and God delivered them and converted the jailer and his family. The church prayed for new believers (Acts 21:5). They prayed for the sick

(Acts 28:8). The unmistakable picture that emerges is that of a church which recognized its dependence upon God and which constantly made prayer a vital part of its life.

Unity. The sense of unity that prevailed in the early church was remarkable: "And all who believed were together and had all things in common; and they sold their possessions and goods and distributed them to all, as any had need" (Acts 2:44-45). "Now the company of those who believed were of one heart and soul, and no one said that any of the things which he possessed was his own, but they had everything in common. . . . There was not a needy person among them, for as many as were possessors of lands or houses sold them, and brought the proceeds of what was sold and laid it at the apostles' feet; and distribution was made to each as any had need" (Acts 4:32, 34-35).

The early apostles experienced true unity. As a result it was said of them: "With great power the apostles gave their testimony to the resurrection of the Lord Jesus, and great grace was upon them all" (Acts 4:33). Their unity was the practical outworking of a doctrine which had not yet been fully expounded for them, the doctrine of the body of Christ. Paul develops this in his epistles—the interdependence of the body, each member relying on the other members for a unified functioning of the whole.

This unity as explained by Paul is the ideal, but unfortunately it did not describe the actual situation in the church at Corinth. Paul had to develop the teaching for them because of the disunity apparent in the church. "It has been reported to me. . .that there is quarreling among you, my brethren" (1 Cor. 1:11). Some claimed to follow Peter, others Paul, others Apollos, others Christ; brother was going to law against brother (1 Cor. 6); some were offended by the actions of others (1 Cor. 8). Against this backdrop Paul describes how the body of

Christ (composed of all believers) must function in harmony (1 Cor. 12).

strategy of the early church

The church, characterized by these qualities, had a definite strategy in its outreach. They did not sit down and hammer out methods in committee before beginning to witness. Rather their strategy was developed in the normal everyday process of sharing their faith with others who did not know Jesus Christ. A study of the New Testament reveals certain elements that contributed to an overall strategy and which can serve as a pattern for the church today.

Witness of All Believers. In the New Testament we do not find the cleavage between clergy and laymen that sprang up in later centuries. While some were clearly designated by God for special ministry of the Word (cf. Acts 6:2-4), all Christians participated in witnessing for Jesus Christ. This is spelled out in Acts 8 where we read that "they were all scattered throughout the region of Judea and Samaria, *except the apostles* . . . . Now those who were scattered went about preaching the word" (Acts 8:1, 4). That is, those who were *not* apostles were preaching the Word wherever they went.

Presumably the Ethiopian eunuch took the gospel to his own land (Acts 8). In fact, the Coptic Church of Ethiopia today claims to be his spiritual descendent. Ananias was not an apostle, but God chose him to bring Saul of Tarsus to an understanding of the gospel (Acts 9). Dorcas, an unknown seamstress, was "full of good works and acts of charity" (Acts 9:36) which were part of her witness. Aquila and Priscilla, humble tentmakers, took the eloquent Apollos and "expounded to him the way of God more accurately" (Acts 18:26).

It was through this involvement of every believer that the church expanded so rapidly. Strachan emphasizes this when he says, "The apostolic strategy was to involve every Christian in constant responsible service and witness in every situation of secular and religious life."[5]

Today this concept is being grasped anew by the church around the world. New recognition of the place of the layman in the witness of the church has spurred a revitalizing movement of lay leadership. This is basic to the theorem underlying "Evangelism-in-Depth": "The expansion of any movement is in direct proportion to its success in mobilizing its total membership in continuous propagation of its beliefs."[6]

This is a concept conceived by Kenneth Strachan and developed by the churches in Latin America. It attempts to mobilize all the manpower in every local church in an entire nation to reach out with the gospel to every person. To date it has grown with increasing success through nationwide efforts in ten Latin American republics. Similar movements have sprung up around the world, some indebted to Latin America for the concept, some quite spontaneously and independently. Everywhere the emphasis has been on total mobilization of all believers for total outreach. Instead of multiplying the hearers in an evangelistic campaign, it multiplies the evangelists by making every believer a witness. The "man in the pew" becomes the one preaching the Word, while the preacher cooperates in his training.

Recognition of Gifts of the Spirit. As Christians became active in the witness of the church, they learned to recognize the gifts given by the Holy Spirit. Consequently, they were willing to accept responsibilities, no matter how menial the task seemed, in accord with those gifts. Some were called to devote themselves "to prayer and to the ministry of the

---

[5] Strachan, p. 64.
[6] *Ibid.*, p. 108.

word," while others were chosen "to serve tables" (Acts 6:2-4). Paul emphasized that "the eye cannot say to the hand, 'I have no need of you,' nor again the head to the feet, 'I have no need of you.' On the contrary, the parts of the body which seem to be weaker are indispensable . . . that there may be no discord in the body, but that the members may have the same care for one another" (1 Cor. 12:21-22, 25).

The New Testament records the names of many obscure people who became "hands" and "feet" to the apostle Paul. "Phoebe . . . has been a helper of many and of myself as well" (Rom. 16:1-2). "Prisca and Aquila . . . risked their necks for my life" (Rom. 16:3). "Mary . . . has worked hard among you" (Rom. 16:6). "Persis . . . has worked hard in the Lord" (Rom. 16:12). "Gaius . . . is host to me and to the whole church" (Rom. 16:23). "The household of Stephanas . . . have devoted themselves to the service of the saints. . . . Stephanas and Fortunatus and Achaicus . . . refreshed my spirit as well as yours" (1 Cor. 16:15-18). "I have no one like him [Timothy] . . . . As a son with a father he has served with me in the gospel" (Phil. 2:19-22). "Epaphroditus my brother and fellow worker and fellow soldier, and your messenger and minister to my need" (Phil. 2:25). "Epaphras our beloved fellow servant . . . a faithful minister of Christ on our behalf" (Col. 1:7). "Tychicus . . . a beloved brother and faithful minister and fellow servant in the Lord" (Col. 4:7). "Luke the beloved physician" (Col. 4:14). "Mark . . . is very useful in serving me" (2 Tim. 4:11). "Onesimus, whose father I have become in my imprisonment. (Formerly he was useless to you, but now he is indeed useful to you and to me)" (Philem. 10-11).

These are the unsung saints who were willing to accept their ministry in the body of Christ, no matter how insignificant their work might have appeared. They are not without their reward.

Constant Preaching of the Word. The involvement of every Christian in outreach plus the recognition of the gifts that differ within the church were the natural setting for a constant proclamation of the message of salvation. This was done to individuals (Philip to the eunuch), to families (Peter to Cornelius, Paul to the Philippian jailer), to religious and political authorities (Peter before the Sanhedrin, Paul before Felix and Festus), in the synagogue (Paul in Antioch of Pisidia), in the marketplace (Paul in Athens and on the Areopagus), in homes (Paul in Rome), in the church (whenever Paul established a church), in school (Paul in the school of Tyrannus) and at work (Aquila and Priscilla to Apollos). In other words, wherever the Christians could find an audience—one person or a great multitude—they were quick to speak of Jesus and the resurrection.

It was every Christian's constant propagation of belief that explains why within three centuries the Roman Empire was forced to recognize this movement as the leading religion of the empire. "Nothing is clearer than that this missionary enterprise, as set forth in The Acts and conceived by the apostolic church, was no side issue, no secondary affair, not merely one of a number of equally important, or unimportant, things; it was the primary thing, the main drive, the supreme object in view which took precedence over everything else."[7]

Service to Those in Need. This preaching and witnessing, however, was never carried out in isolation from the physical and material needs of the people. We have noted above how the believers had all things in common and shared their goods so that no one lacked. They healed the sick, they raised the dead, they cast out demons. When the widows were neglected, deacons were appointed to serve them (Acts 6:1-7). When Paul

---

[7]Glover, pp. 33-34.

saw a helpless demon-possessed girl being used gainfully by an unscrupulous profiteer, Paul cast out the demon and brought down the ire of her masters (Acts 16:16-24). When the Christians in Jerusalem were suffering for lack of the necessities of life, the churches in Macedonia and Achaia, out of their own poverty, took an offering and sent it with Paul to help out their brothers in Jerusalem (Rom. 15:25-27; 2 Cor. 8:1-4). When Paul was in prison, men like Epaphroditus ministered to his needs (Phil. 2:25-29), and the church in Philippi sent gifts to help him (Phil. 4:18).

Thus there was a genuine concern for men's total needs—physical as well as spiritual. And this concern, while expressed especially within the church, was not confined to the church. Paul exhorts the church in Galatia, "So then, as we have opportunity, let us do good to all men, and especially to those who are of the household of faith" (Gal. 6:10).

Use of Strategic Centers. The pattern that Paul employed in his constant efforts to preach the gospel in new regions was to use strategic centers. He usually went to an important city of the empire. Sometimes the city was on a major highway or served as a key port in the east-west trade of Rome. He aimed at centers such as Athens, Corinth and even Rome itself, believing that if the gospel could take root there, it would then expand out in concentric circles through the surrounding region. And the gospel spread. After Paul spent two years in Ephesus, it could be said that "all the residents of Asia heard the word of the Lord, both Jews and Greeks" (Acts 19:10). To the Christians in the key city of Thessalonica Paul could write, "For not only has the word of the Lord sounded forth from you in Macedonia and Achaia, but your faith in God has gone forth everywhere, so that we need not say anything" (1 Thess. 1:8).

Training of Disciples. It was noted in Chapter 2 that the

imperative in the Great Commission as given in Matthew was to "make disciples." Paul did precisely this. He chose young men with potential who could be with him to learn from him so that they could later assume broader responsibilities and train others. Paul writes to Timothy, who had spent much time with Paul in his travels, "What you have heard from me before many witnesses entrust to faithful men who will be able to teach others also" (2 Tim. 2:2).

Paul himself was the product of one who had discipled him in a personal way. When Paul first arrived in Jerusalem, friendless and under suspicion of the Christians whom he had previously persecuted, Barnabas took him under his wing and vouched for him before the Christians. Undoubtedly Barnabas helped to instruct him in the truths of salvation.

Paul's best-known disciple was Timothy to whom he wrote two letters of instruction. However, he trained many other men as well. He left Titus in Crete to build up the new church there and then wrote an epistle to instruct him in his ministry. He wrote to Philemon to instruct him in helping a new convert, Onesimus, formerly a slave of Philemon. He sent Epaphroditus to the Colossians. Silas, Luke and others accompanied Paul on his second missionary journey. Silvanus and Timothy joined Paul in writing the two letters to the church at Thessalonica. Many of the obscure Christians mentioned above were disciples whom Paul had instructed in the Christian life.

Follow-up of New Believers. Paul never left the young churches without help. He employed at least four means to cultivate them in their newly found faith. First, he prayed regularly for them, "I thank my God in all my remembrance of you, always in every prayer of mine for you all making my prayer with joy" (Phil. 1:3-4). "And so, from the day we heard of it, we have not ceased to pray for you" (Col. 1:9).

Second, he visited them personally whenever possible. On

all three of his missionary journeys he returned to places he had visited previously, either on the same trip or on a previous one. His second journey was undertaken when Paul said to Barnabas, "Come, let us return and visit the brethren in every city where we proclaimed the word of the Lord, and see how they are" (Acts 15:36).

Third, when he could not visit personally, he sometimes sent someone else in his place. He told the Christians at Philippi, "I hope in the Lord Jesus to send Timothy to you soon. . . . I have no one like him, who will be genuinely anxious for your welfare" (Phil. 2:19-20). He left Titus in Crete that he might lead forward the young church there (Titus 1:5).

Fourth, he followed up many previous contacts by letter. Nine of Paul's letters were addressed to young churches, most of which he had established himself. In writing to the Corinthians Paul dealt directly and boldly with the problems which they were facing as a new church: disunity, spiritual immaturity, immorality, brother going to law against a brother, separation from idolatry, questions of conscience (meat offered to idols), celebration of the Lord's supper, the dress of women, spiritual gifts and their use and control in the church, love, the hope of the resurrection, and the collection of an offering.

To the Galatians he gave exhortations not to be led astray by confusing or enticing doctrines and helped them understand the relationship between the law of the Old Testament and the grace of Jesus Christ. To the Ephesians he explained the place of the Christian who is in Christ. Then he gave very practical instructions for home life (relations between husbands and wives, fathers and children, masters and servants), ending up by describing the Christian's armor.

To the Colossians who were confused by mystical philosophies of the east he wrote of the supremacy of Jesus

Christ. To the Thessalonians he wrote of the coming of Christ, then followed with a second letter to clarify questions which had been raised by the first letter.

Paul also sent four letters to friends whom he wished to instruct further in the Lord. Timothy and Titus were both young companions who were helping Paul in the ministry. He told them how to behave in their churches, how to choose elders and deacons, how to face the apostasy which would come and how to be an example to the believers.

The personal touch of follow-up was a key part of Paul's strategy.

Thus, the church is God's instrument for the furtherance of the gospel. It is to the church that he has entrusted the ministry of reconciliation. Being composed of human beings who are still sinners, the church has never been perfect. But the New Testament gives us a picture of the characteristics and strategy which should be employed in fulfilling the Great Commission which Jesus Christ left to the church. The standards are high, but he has not left us alone. He has given to us his Holy Spirit and his promise, "Lo, I am with you always, to the close of the age" (Mt. 28:20).

PART II: THE HISTORICAL PERSPECTIVE

chapter 5

early beginnings

acts unfinished

The book of Acts is, in a sense, unfinished. It begins by referring to "all that Jesus began to do and teach" (as recorded in the gospels) and ends abruptly with Paul in Rome. Apparently no attempt was made to bring the book to a conclusion. It was recognized that the work of the Holy Spirit in spreading the gospel would go on continuously through the church and throughout the world.

The next three centuries were to see the most phenomenal spread of Christianity that could be imagined. After Constantine (274-337 A.D.) the church, now secure in its position in the Roman Empire, seemed to lose much of its missionary zeal. However, the following centuries are not devoid of stories of committed men, often working alone, who tirelessly carried the message of salvation to other parts of the world. While the history of the expansion of Christianity through the first fifteen centuries of its existence is a saga replete with drama and excitement, it is not the purpose of this book to trace that history. This has been done elsewhere by competent scholars.[1] Rather it is our purpose to see how students have had a direct influence in the missionary outreach of the church.

It is remarkable that students have played a decisive role in many of the greatest forward movements of the church in world evangelism. It has been through their vision and energy that the church has often been propelled into renewed efforts of outreach. In order to set in historical perspective the place of today's students in the world mission of the church, we need to see the rich heritage left by former generations of students.

earliest traces

Perhaps the earliest traceable instance in which students had a definite part in promoting a world outreach is found in Germany in the early seventeenth century. Gustav Warneck, the great historian-theologian of missions, writes of seven young law students from Lubeck, Germany, who, while studying together in Paris, committed themselves to carry the gospel overseas. At least three of them finally sailed for Africa. All trace has been lost of two of these, but the name of Peter Heiling has survived. After a two-year stay in Egypt, he proceded to Abyssinia in 1634. He spent some twenty years in that land, where he translated the Bible into Amharic and finally died a martyr.[2]

---

[1] For those who wish to pursue the history of Christian missions in more detail the following works are suggested: Stephen Neill, *A History of Christian Missions* (Baltimore: Penguin Books, 1964); Kenneth Scott Latourette, *A History of the Expansion of Christianity* (New York: Harper and Brothers), 7 volumes, 1937-45.

[2] Gustav Warneck, *History of Protestant Missions* (London: Oliphant, Anderson, and Ferrier, 1901), p. 25.

Heiling had no successors, and thus there was no continuation of what he began. But the translation of the Scriptures was a significant contribution that unquestionably made its impact. The important thing to note here is that his original impetus to leave his own land and carry the gospel to another part of the world came when he banded together with fellow students to pray and work for the extension of the church overseas.

the moravians

The name of Count Nicolaus Ludwig von Zinzendorf (1700-1760) stands high in missionary annals as a leader of the Moravian movement, one of the first, most effective and most enduring of missionary enterprises. Raised in the home of aristocratic Lutherans who were followers of the Pietist movement, Zinzendorf had the good fortune to know personally both Spener and Francke, the great leaders of the Pietists. The emphasis on a personal relationship to Jesus Christ as Lord became the most influential factor in his early life. "I have but one passion . . . 'tis He, 'tis only He," he wrote.[3] Before the age of ten he had determined that his lifelong purpose should be to preach the gospel of Jesus Christ throughout the world.[4]

From 1710 to 1716, Zinzendorf studied in the Paedagogium founded by Francke in Halle, Germany. Here he wielded an unusual influence among his fellow students through the purity of his personal life and his passion for Jesus Christ and his desire to make Christ known to others.

With five other boys he formed the Order of the Grain of Mustard Seed. This was sort of a spiritual secret society whose

---

[3] Arthur J. Lewis, *Zinzendorf, The Ecumenical Pioneer* (Philadelphia: Westminster Press, 1962), p. 12.

[4] *Ibid.*, p. 24.

members were bound together in prayer. Their purposes were to witness to the power of Jesus Christ, to draw other Christians together in fellowship regardless of their ecclesiastical connections, to help those who were suffering for their faith and to carry the gospel of Christ to those overseas who had not yet heard the message.[5] Thus, it was as a student that Zinzendorf first took steps to spread the gospel to other parts of the world. This same vision was carried over in his university days at Wittenberg and Utrecht. He never lost sight of this purpose.

In April, 1731, Zinzendorf attended the coronation of Christian VI of Denmark in Copenhagen. There he met Anthony Ulrich, from St. Thomas in the West Indies, who shared with the Count his deep desire that his brothers in the West Indies should hear the gospel. So deeply impressed was Zinzendorf with this need that he saw the relationship between this and the commitments he had made as a student to carry the gospel overseas. By August, 1732, arrangements had been made for the first two Moravian missionaries to sail for St. Thomas.

Thus, the modern worldwide missionary movement (which traces parts of its roots to the Moravians of 1732) was actually born in the hearts of a group of students who joined together at Halle to pray for world evangelism.

the wesleys

At the same time God was at work in the life of Zinzendorf and his companions in Germany, he was also moving among students in England. Charles Wesley entered Christ Church College, Oxford, in 1726, from which his brother, John, had just graduated. Because of his desire to know God better, he

---

[5] *Ibid.*, pp. 25-26.

soon formed a small society of students for the study of the classics and the New Testament. They became known as the "Holy Club" (in derision from their fellow students) and as the "Methodists" (because of their methodical approach to life). John Wesley returned as a teaching fellow to Lincoln College at Oxford and joined his brother in the activities of this group.

In addition to worship and study the group translated their piety into an outreach to the poor, the hungry and the imprisoned. This facet of their activities became an increasingly important part of their club.

While John Wesley is usually known as an evangelist and theologian and Charles as a hymn writer, they both began their fruitful careers as overseas missionaries. In October, 1735, the two brothers sailed for the colony of Georgia with General Oglethorpe. John Wesley's journal indicates that he was not yet sure of his own salvation at this point and that his sailing for Georgia was partly a quest for knowing God better. At the same time he had the desire to share what he knew of Christ with the Indians of America.

Shortly after Wesley arrived in Georgia, the English colonists there tried to persuade him to remain in Savannah as their pastor. However, his desire to preach the gospel to the unevangelized Indians caused him to write in his journal:

Tuesday, November 23 (1736)–Mr. Oglethorpe sailed for England, leaving Mr. Ingham, Mr. Delamotte, and me at Savannah, but with less prospect of preaching to the Indians than we had the first day we set foot in America. Whenever I mentioned it, it was immediately replied, "You cannot leave Savannah without a minister."

To this indeed my plain answer was, "I know not that I am under any obligation to the contrary. I never promised to stay here one month. I openly declared both before, at, and ever since, my coming hither that I neither would nor could take charge of the English any longer than till I could go among the Indians."[6]

This desire to share the message of Christianity with the Indians who did not know Jesus Christ was apparently a direct outgrowth of the fellowship of students at Oxford who sought to know God better through their "Holy Club."

charles simeon

No summary of the movement of God among students in England would be complete without reference to Charles Simeon. As a student at Cambridge University in 1779, Simeon came to know Christ. Following his graduation in 1882, he was appointed Fellow of King's College, ordained to the ministry and named incumbent of the Holy Trinity Church at Cambridge. Thus began a remarkable ministry that was to span fifty-four years.

Students who came under Simeon's influence in Cambridge later became some of the great leaders of the church both in Great Britain and around the world. His informal gatherings of undergraduates in his home for Bible study and prayer were perhaps the most influential part of his work. Here scores of students first came to a personal relationship to Jesus Christ. Here they began to understand the Word of God and its implications for their lives. And here they received their first visions of reaching out to others with that Word.

This outreach took very practical forms. In 1827, for example, a group of five students, strongly influenced by Simeon's preaching at Holy Trinity Church, formed the Jesus Lane

---

[6] *The Journal of John Wesley*, ed. by Percy Livingston Parker (Chicago: Moody Press, 1951), p. 41.

Sunday School in an attempt to reach the boys and girls of the community with the gospel of Christ. Among those who taught in this Sunday School were men such as Conybeare, Howson, and Westcott, later to be known throughout the world for biblical scholarship.

Another example of outreach in which Simeon had some direct influence was the forming of an auxiliary of the British and Foreign Bible Society at Cambridge in 1811. The purpose of the Society had always been to make available the Word of God throughout the world in the language of the people. The involvement of students in this auxiliary undoubtedly served to broaden their horizons and help them see how they could relate to world evangelism.

One of the most outstanding aspects of Simeon's work at Cambridge was its continuation long after his death in 1836. The "Simeonites" (as the students who attended his informal gatherings were dubbed) continued their activities in the Jesus Lane Sunday School and elsewhere in an outreach with the gospel. In 1848, the Cambridge Union for Private Prayer was formed and became a vital factor in the spiritual life and witness of many.

In 1857, David Livingstone visited Cambridge and delivered a moving and sobering missionary address. Partly as a result of this visit, the Cambridge University Church Missionary Union was established early in 1858 for the purpose of encouraging "a more extended missionary spirit by frequent meetings for prayer and the reading of papers, and for bringing forward an increased number of candidates for missionary employment."[7]

The Inter-Varsity Fellowship of England traces its origins directly to the work begun by Charles Simeon. The Cambridge

---

[7] J. C. Pollock, *A Cambridge Movement* (London: John Murray, 1953), p. 19.

Inter-Collegiate Christian Union was formed in 1877. From small beginnings this movement soon spread to other British universities, then to other countries and finally around the world. Today the International Fellowship of Evangelical Students (IFES) serves as a fraternal link to bind together the local fellowships of students related to such movements as Inter-Varsity Christian Fellowship in its various national forms.

But we have gotten ahead of ourselves.

the cambridge seven

In 1882, the American evangelist, D. L. Moody, visited Cambridge during a tour of Britain. The results of one week of meetings were beyond expectations as a great impact with the gospel was made at the university. While the major purpose of this campaign was evangelistic, J. C. Pollock points out that "it was in the increase of missionary zeal that the impetus given by Moody was the most marked.... Many of Moody's converts were soon sensing a call to the foreign field."[8] Immediately after his visit there was a rapid increase in the number of students who applied to the Church Missionary Society of the Anglican Church for service overseas.

About the same time there was a mounting interest in a new mission, the China Inland Mission, recently founded by J. Hudson Taylor. In 1883-84, a group of seven outstanding students (six of them from Cambridge) applied to the China Inland Mission. They were all brilliant and talented men with good background and upbringing and a variety of athletic and academic abilities.

Montagu H. P. Beauchamp, son of Sir Thomas and Lady Beauchamp, was a brilliant student. William W. Cassels was

---

[8] *Ibid.*, p. 72.

born in Portugal, son of a businessman. After graduation from Cambridge he was ordained curate of the city parish of South Lambeth. Dixon Edward Hoste was converted under D. L. Moody. He held a commission in the Royal Artillery and was later to become the successor of Hudson Taylor as director of the China Inland Mission. Arthur Polhill-Turner was the son of a member of Parliament. Outgoing and quick, he played cricket and made friends easily at Cambridge. He, too, was converted under D. L. Moody. Arthur's brother, Cecil Polhill-Turner, was reserved but very close to Arthur. He was commissioned in the Dragoon Guards. Stanley P. Smith was the son of a successful London surgeon who was unashamedly Christian. Smith, in spite of delicate health, became Captain of First Trinity Boat Club and stroke of the Varsity crew at Cambridge. Although he was brought up in a Christian home, he committed his life to Christ under the ministry of D. L. Moody. Charles Thomas Studd was the son of wealthy parents who knew every luxury of life. At Cambridge he was captain of the cricket team and generally considered the outstanding cricketer of his day.

In a variety of ways the Spirit of God began to move upon each of these men concerning going to China. Slowly but relentlessly the Spirit brought each one to a place of commitment and subsequently to an application for missionary service. Sensing a unity of purpose and outlook, these seven men desired to share their vision of the needs of the world with their fellow students. Following graduation they traveled extensively throughout England and Scotland, visiting the campuses and churches to present the claims of Jesus Christ and the needs of the world for the gospel. Their impact for missionary work was far beyond the few months of time they invested in this tour. In February, 1885, the seven sailed for China, to be followed in subsequent years by scores of students who, under their influence, had given themselves to Jesus Christ to reach other parts of the world that still awaited the gospel.

Thus the forward movement of the church continued to be inspired by youth. Whether it was among students at Halle with Zinzendorf, or at Oxford with the Wesleys, or at Cambridge with C. T. Studd and his fellows, the Holy Spirit continued to use students as spearheads in awakening the church to its worldwide responsibilities.

chapter 6

the haystack movement

the first american missionary

On the North American continent the beginnings of overseas interest on the part of the church can be traced directly to student influence, and more precisely, to the impact of one student, Samuel J. Mills, Jr. (1783-1818). Born in Connecticut as the son of a Congregational minister, Mills was brought up in a godly home. His mother reportedly said of him, "I have consecrated this child to the service of God as a missionary."[1] This was a remarkable statement since missionary interest was practically unknown in the churches of that day, and no channels (such as mission boards) for overseas service existed in America.

Mills was converted at the age of seventeen as a part of the Great Awakening that began in 1798 and touched his father's

---

[1] Watson A. Omulogoli, *The Student Volunteer Movement: Its History and Contribution,* unpublished M.A. thesis, Wheaton College, Wheaton, Ill., 1967, p. 18.

church. His commitment to world evangelism seemed to be an integral part of his conversion experience. From the moment of conversion, on through the years of his study and for the rest of his public ministry, he never lost sight of this purpose.[2]

At the age of nineteen Mills remarked to his father that he could think of no course in life that would be more fulfilling to him than to "communicate the Gospel of Salvation to the poor heathen."[3]

When one reads today, more than a century and a half later, the writings of men like Mills, it would be easy to find fault with their terminology and to criticize them of "paternalism" or, some would even say, "cultural imperialism." Their way of expressing themselves was different from what would be used today and might therefore be misinterpreted. However, when one remembers the limitations of communications, of world understanding and of cultural interchange, it is not surprising that their desire to give the gospel to others might be expressed in terms that today sound paternalistic.

the prayer meeting

In 1806, Mills enrolled in Williams College, Massachusetts. This school had been profoundly affected by the religious awakening of those years, and devout students on campus had a deep concern for the spiritual welfare of their fellow students. Mills joined with them in their desire to help others. Apparently he was unattractive intellectually and physically (he was reported to have "an awkward figure and ungainly manner and an unelastic and croaking sort of voice");[4] yet he became

---

[2] William B. Sprague, *Annals of the American Pulpit* (New York: Robert Larker and Brothers, 1859), p. 556.

[3] Omulogoli, p. 19.

[4] Clarence P. Shedd, *Two Centuries of Student Christian Movements* (New York: Association Press, 1934), p. 49-50.

much sought after by students who were convicted of sin and realized their need of spiritual counsel.

It was Mills' custom to spend Wednesday and Saturday afternoons in prayer with other students on the banks of the Hoosack River or in a valley near the college. In August, 1806, Mills and four others were caught in a thunderstorm while returning from their usual meeting. Seeking refuge under a haystack they waited out the storm and gave themselves to prayer. Their special focus of prayer that day was for the awakening of foreign missionary interest among students. Mills directed their discussion and prayer to their own missionary obligation. He exhorted his companions with the words that later became a watchword for them, "We can do this if we will."

"Bowed in prayer, these first American student volunteers for foreign missions willed that God should have their lives for service wherever he needed them, and in that self-dedication really gave birth to the first student missionary society in America."[5] Kenneth Scott Latourette, the foremost historian of the church's worldwide expansion, states, "It was from this haystack meeting that the foreign missionary movement of the churches of the United States had an initial main impulse."[6]

The exact location of the haystack was unknown for a number of years. Then, in 1854, Bryan Green, one of those present in 1806, visited Williamstown and located the spot. A monument was erected on the sight in 1867. Mark Hopkins, who was then president of the American Board of Commissioners for Foreign Missions, gave the dedicatory address in

---

[5] *Ibid.*, p. 52.
[6] Kenneth Scott Latourette, *These Sought a Country* (New York: Harper and Brothers, 1950), p. 46.

which he said, "For once in the history of the world a prayer meeting is commemorated by a monument."[7]

the society of brethren
Back at Williams College these students, along with others of like mind, continued to meet regularly for prayer and for world evangelism. They were influential in leading a number of other students into a commitment of their lives for overseas service. In September, 1808, deciding to organize formally, they founded The Society of the Brethren. Their members were bound together by an oath of secrecy and the purpose of giving themselves to extend the gospel around the world.

Desiring to extend the influence of this Society to other colleges, one of their members transferred to Middlebury College to found a similar society there. In 1809, following his graduation from Williams College, Mills enrolled at Yale with the dual purpose of continuing theological studies and of imparting missionary vision to the students there.

Here he met Henry Obookiah, a Hawaiian, who encouraged him with the need of evangelizing the Hawaiian Islands. Obookiah did much in the next few years to stimulate student interest in evangelizing the Pacific Islands. He died prematurely before he was able to return to his homeland, but Latourette says of him, "The story of his life and missionary purpose was a major stimulus to the sending, in 1819, the year after his death, of the first missionaries of the American Board to Hawaii."[8] (James Michener's caricature of Abner Hale as the first missionary to Hawaii, in his novel *Hawaii,* should not be allowed to obscure the commitment which led Obookiah,

---

[7] *The Haystack Centennial* (Boston: American Board of Commissioners for Foreign Missions, 1907), p. 216.

[8] Latourette, p. 51.

Mills and other students to be concerned for the evangelization of those who had never heard of Christ.)

the american board of commissioners for foreign missions

In June, 1810, the General Association of Congregational Churches met in Bradford, Massachusetts, in annual meeting. Samuel Mills (then studying at Andover Theological Seminary), with several fellow students, including Adoniram Judson, presented a petition requesting the formation of a society which could send them out as foreign missionaries. Up to this date no such organization existed. The petition was originally signed by six students, but the signatures were reduced to four "for fear of alarming the Association with too large a number."[9] The petition was received on June 28, 1810. On June 29, the Association recommended to the assembly "That there be instituted by this General Association a Board of Commissioners for Foreign Missions, for the purpose of devising ways and means, and adopting and prosecuting measures, for promoting the spread of the Gospel to heathen lands."[10] (One could wish that ecclesiastical circles could move as rapidly today!) Although not legally incorporated until 1812, the Board began activities immediately. It was interdenominational in character, enjoying the support of numerous church bodies. Volunteers were recruited and prepared.

On February 19, 1812, Adoniram Judson and Samuel Newell and their wives sailed for India, and five days later Samuel Nott, Gordon Hall and Luther Rice also embarked on another ship for India. These first American missionaries join-

---

[9] *Memorial Volume of the First Fifty Years* (Boston: American Board of Commissioners for Foreign Missions, 1861), p. 43.

[10] Joseph Tracy, *History of the American Board of Commissioners for Foreign Missions* (New York: M. W. Dodd, 1842), p. 26.

ed hands with the great English pioneer, William Carey, who since 1793 had been evangelizing in India. Judson and Rice subsequently persuaded the Baptists of North America to form their own missionary society which became the second foreign board in the United States.

Thus, within four years of the haystack prayer meeting, these students had been influential in the formation of the first North American missionary society, and a year and a half later the first volunteers were on their way to Asia.

missions and social concern

In this age it is popular to criticize foreign missions for failure to be concerned sufficiently with the social and physical needs of people. Hollywood, modern literature and current journalists have often portrayed the missionary as one who seeks only the soul of man and forgets about his physical needs.

However, anyone who will take the time to study the legacy of Samuel J. Mills will be impressed with the breadth of his concerns and activities. For Mills there was no false dichotomy between "home" and "foreign" missions. Nor did he engage in fruitless debate about the relative merits of "evangelism" as distinct from "social service." For him it was not a question of "either-or" but "both-and." In addition to spearheading the founding of the first mission board, Mills took an active part in a variety of other concerns.

In 1816, he participated in the establishing of the American Bible Society, a movement whose influence in the spread of the gospel through the dissemination of the written Word of God will only be evaluated in eternity.

During the summer of 1816, Mills worked in the urban slums, or ghettos, of New York City, being deeply moved by the needs of poverty-stricken people who were trapped there. His journal written during that summer depicts untiring efforts to reach the underprivileged peoples of New York with the message of salvation. These were accompanied by equal endeavors to help alleviate physical suffering. And through all his records runs the thread of his continued interest in spreading the gospel, with its healing influence, around the world. [11]

Mills also became concerned with the welfare of the seamen who came by the thousands into the port of New York. Consequently, he helped to found the Marine Bible Society for the purpose of evangelizing these seamen.

Mills was detained from sailing overseas with his companions in 1812 because the Board wanted him to help in two major endeavors: first, to stimulate further missionary interest among the churches in America and second, to help explore the missionary possibilities among the Indians of the western frontier of the United States. During the next few years Mills made several trips to the Mississippi valley, the principal purpose being "to preach the Gospel to the destitute, to ascertain the moral and religious wants of the country, and to form Bible societies and other religious and benevolent institutions." [12] In fact, missions to the Indians became a major concern for him during these years.

Perhaps Mills' most intriguing vision was one which could be called his crowning glory, for it was while pursuing this vision that he met death. Being concerned for world evangelism, he looked toward Africa. Then, being equally concerned for the plight of the downtrodden, he looked at the slaves of the United States. Putting these two together, he helped to found the American Colonization Society on January 1, 1817. The purpose of this Society was to evangelize the slaves in America, work toward their liberation and then repatriate

[11] Sprague, p. 568.
[12] Tracy, p. 567.

them to Africa. He saw that these blacks could be raised from their miserable condition of slavery and at the same time could be the best possible missionaries to their own people of Africa.

He devoted more time to this endeavor in his later years than to any other work. During his trips through the south and to the Mississippi valley, he became deeply impressed with the importance of this goal and of the responsibility of American Christians to it. He considered no sacrifice too great, including death itself if necessary, to help fulfill this goal.[13]

In November, 1817, Mills went to Africa to survey lands—in what is now Liberia—for use in this program of repatriation. While returning to America, he contracted an illness and died at sea on June 15, 1818, at the age of thirty-five. Less than twelve years had passed since this amazing young man had knelt with his companions under the haystack near the Hoosack River. Yet in that short time he had formed The Society of Brethren, stimulated the founding of the first foreign mission board from North America, participated in sending the first missionaries, worked toward the betterment of the poverty-stricken in the ghettos of New York, helped found two Bible societies, ministered to the Indians of the Mississippi valley and finally gave his life in the effort to break the chains of slaves in America and combine this with the evangelization of Africa. Not a minor accomplishment.

[13] Sprague, p. 568.

chapter 7

from haystack to mt. hermon

student missionary societies

The nineteenth century saw the rise of many strong religious organizations and movements. Not the least of these were movements that had their roots in the students of the day. The awakening of missionary zeal was accompanied by a general awakening of spiritual vigor among students. What happened through the haystack group had its effect on other groups of students across the country. The missionary interest fomented through these groups led directly to the creation of the intercollegiate YMCA and YWCA with the Student Volunteer Movement as their channel for missionary activity.[1]

The Society of Brethren founded at Williams College by the students from the haystack group was to have a vast and worldwide influence. In 1810, the Society was established at Andover, which became the base of its operation for the next sixty years. During this period 527 students joined the Society and about fifty per cent of them actually went overseas as missionaries.[2]

---

[1] Shedd, pp. 59-60.
[2] *Ibid.*, p. 62.

the society of inquiry
In 1811, another body was formed at Andover which was to have perhaps an even greater influence for foreign missions. It was called "The Society of Inquiry on the Subject of Missions." Its purpose and scope were not in conflict with those of the Society of Brethren, so seven of the nine charter members, including Samuel J. Mills, were members of both groups. This society had a long and distinguished history, lasting more than one hundred years. Its purposes were primarily informative and educational—collecting and disseminating information on the needs of the world and the church's responsibility to meet these needs.

This society was influential in stirring up churches and colleges to consider their worldwide responsibilities. Between 1810 and 1850, most of the student religious groups that were organized adopted a missionary character and most of them took the name of Society of Inquiry or Society of Inquiry on Behalf of Missions.[3]

So pronounced was this missionary activity among students that the establishment of Societies of Inquiry became widespread by the middle of the nineteenth century. In 1856, there were 156 colleges and 46 theological seminaries in the United States. Seventy of these colleges had Christian societies of one sort or another (theological, devotional or missionary in emphasis). Of these, 49 had societies which included in their title "Society of Inquiry" to designate foreign missionary emphasis.[4]

the ymca
On June 6, 1844, the Young Men's Christian Association was

---

[3] *Ibid.*, p. 65.
[4] *Ibid.*, pp. 69-73.

formed in London under the leadership of a dry goods merchant, George Williams, who was concerned for the spiritual welfare of young men in the big city. In 1851, the YMCA was organized on the North American continent in Montreal and Boston.

The major emphasis of the YMCA at that time was evangelistic, including welfare and relief services as a vital part of the preaching of the gospel. Strategically located rooms became centers for libraries, lecture courses and social activities. The spiritual and moral welfare of young men adrift in the big cities was their chief concern. So rapid was the growth of this movement across North America that within three years there was a YMCA in virtually every major city as well as in many smaller ones.[5]

As early as 1856, YMCA's were beginning to appear on the college campuses as well as in the cities. These were related to the revivals of the 1850's. Students at the University of Michigan formed a YMCA in 1856, formally adopting a constitution in February, 1858. However, this group did not join the national movement until after the Civil War. At the University of Virginia a YMCA was formed in 1856, adopting a constitution in October, 1858. This group may be regarded as the most significant student YMCA in America before the Civil War.[6]

Similar movements were spreading across the country on campuses, fomenting for the next twenty years a growing desire for the formation of a college division of the YMCA. This was culminated at the Louisville convention in June, 1877, when Luther Wishard was appointed Corresponding Secretary

---

[5] C. Howard Hopkins, *History of the Y.M.C.A. in North America* (New York: Association Press, 1951), p. 15. I am indebted to this volume for much of the material on the YMCA.

[6] *Ibid.*, p. 37.

to direct the work of the YMCA in higher educational institutions at a salary of $250 per year.

Wishard (1854-1925) had been active in YMCA at Hanover College and Princeton. He came to his new work with a great vision to unite the work in all the colleges, the ultimate goal being the conversion of students and their commitment to active Christian service. His efforts for the next eleven years (during seven years he was the only student Christian movement secretary in the world) were tireless and extensive. Strong emphasis was laid on personal prayer life and Bible study, evangelism and social outreach in the neighborhood near the campus.

For the purposes of this study the most significant thing to note about Wishard is that his "program was soon focused upon foreign missions, and out of it there grew a student missionary movement unparalleled in the history of Christianity."[7]

The most important development during Wishard's first year was his personal commitment to the cause of foreign missions. In connection with this he conceived the idea of a world student fellowship. These two causes became the outstanding features of the student department of the YMCA for the next several decades and also its largest contribution to the church throughout the world. When Wishard heard of what took place at Williams College in 1806, he saw at once that what was happening in his day was a renewal of the same spirit: " 'What they had done was ours to complete.' He was himself, as Mott later said, 'a flame of fire' spreading this great ideal."[8]

In his desire to carry on the heritage handed down from the haystack group, Wishard went to Williams College and "knelt

[7] *Ibid.*, p. 272.
[8] *Ibid.*, p. 280.

in the snow at the Haystack Monument and made 'an unreserved surrender to the great Leader of those earlier volunteers: I am willing to go anywhere at any time to do anything for Jesus.' "[9]

While Wishard keenly wanted to go overseas himself, he became convinced that for the present time he could make more impact by remaining in the United States to bring about a missionary uprising and thus reproduce himself many times over throughout the world. The missionary cause became the center of his work in which all his other activities converged.

the princeton foreign missionary society

One of the individuals who was caught up in the waves of influence that emanated from the haystack prayer meeting was a student named Royal G. Wilder. While studying at Andover in the 1840's, he joined the Society of Brethren and soon was looking toward overseas missionary service. In 1846, Wilder sailed for India under the American Board of Commissioners for Foreign Missions, serving there for the next thirty years. In 1877, he was forced by poor health to return to the United States, where he took up residence in Princeton, New Jersey. Here he founded and edited a periodical, *The Missionary Review of the World*.

His son, Robert P. Wilder, who had been born in Kolhapur, India, in 1863, enrolled in Princeton College in 1881. He proved to be a brilliant student who excelled particularly in Greek and philosophy. He was later elected into Phi Beta Kappa, which did not exist at Princeton during his undergraduate days.

In the autumn of 1883, Robert Wilder and two of his companions attended a conference of the Inter-Seminary Alliance

---

[9] *Ibid.*, p. 282.

in Hartford, Connecticut. Here he heard Dr. A. J. Gordon whose powerful messages on the Holy Spirit made a great impact on the students. Wilder later wrote:

> We three college students returned to Princeton inspired with the desire to accomplish two things: First, to pray and work for a revival in our college, and, second, to stir up missionary interest. We prevailed on like-minded students to form groups, usually consisting of three or four, who met daily at the noon hour. Afterwards we did personal work with those for whom we had prayed. [10]

As a direct result of this, Wilder and his friends formed the Princeton Foreign Missionary Society on the campus of Princeton College in the fall of 1883. The constitution stated:

> The object of this Society shall be the cultivation of a missionary spirit among the students of the College, the information of its members in all subjects of missionary interest, and especially the leading of men to consecrate themselves to foreign missionary work. . . . Any student of the College who is a professing Christian may become a member by subscribing to the following covenant: We, the undersigned, declare ourselves willing and desirous, God permitting, to go to the unevangelized portions of the world. [11]

This group met on Sunday afternoons in the Wilder home for prayer and discussion of missionary needs. While these men met in the parlor, Robert's sister, Grace, a recent graduate of Mt. Holyoke College, prayed for them alone in another room of the home. During the school year of 1885-1886, Robert

---

[10] Robert P. Wilder, *The Student Volunteer Movement: Its Origin and Early History* (New York: The Student Volunteer Movement, 1935), p. 9.

[11] *Ibid.*, pp. 7-8.

and Grace Wilder met together regularly "to pray for a widespread missionary movement in the colleges and universities of America. We asked that ultimately one thousand volunteers might be secured to labor in foreign fields." [12]

The ground was being prepared by God to bring together a host of strands that would bind the haystack prayer meeting, the YMCA, the Princeton movement and, indirectly, even the Cambridge Seven into what has been called "the golden chain stretching from the Haystack Meeting to the greatest student uprising in all history." [13]

---

[12] *Ibid.*, pp. 12-13.
[13] Hopkins, p. 298.

chapter 8

the student volunteer movement for foreign missions

the mt. hermon conference

The first links of that "golden chain" were forged under the haystack in 1806. New links were added during the next eighty years. Then, in 1886, the final links were drawn together to make a mighty chain that was to circle the globe.

In the summer of 1885, Luther Wishard persuaded the evangelist, D. L. Moody, to plan a summer Bible study conference for students to be held the following year at Moody's conference grounds, Mt. Hermon, Massachusetts. With Moody's permission Wishard sent out a circular inviting students to spend the month of July, 1886, studying the Bible under D. L. Moody at Mt. Hermon.

Wishard and his associate, Charles Ober, traveled personally to many campuses to recruit students for the conference. At Princeton Wishard found a ready response from Robert Wilder who, through the activities of the Princeton Foreign Missionary Society, had been well prepared for just such a venture. Although Wilder at first demurred, because he was no longer a student, having just graduated, Wishard insisted on his attending, and he complied.

Before leaving, my sister said to me: "I believe our prayers will be answered at Mt. Hermon and that there our Princeton beginnings will become intercollegiate." She also prophesied, as I remember it, that there would be a hundred volunteers enlisted there.[1]

Charles Ober recruited a student at Cornell named John R. Mott, who was then the vice president of the Cornell chapter of the YMCA. Mott had been profoundly influenced in his spiritual life through the YMCA, and especially through J. E. K. Studd's visit to Cornell in 1885. Studd had gone to the United States to tour campuses and tell of the Cambridge Seven (which included his brother, C. T. Studd). With the help of men like Wilder and Mott, a total of 251 students from eighty-nine colleges and universities of the United States and Canada were recruited to attend the conference.[2]

The conference opened at Mt. Hermon with D. L. Moody announcing that they had no program planned but rather would be emphasizing the Bible and music as "the two important agencies with which to reach the world."[3] He wanted the students to interact with him and with each other in an atmosphere of freedom in the study of the Bible and in the use of music as a means of communicating the gospel. It was a leisurely conference with many meetings held out under the trees.

---

[1] Wilder, p. 9.

[2] John R. Mott, *Five Decades and a Forward View* (New York: Harper and Brothers, 1939), p. 3.

[3] Ruth Wilder Braisted, *In This Generation: The Story of Robert P. Wilder* (New York: Friendship Press, 1941), p. 23.

During the first two weeks, there was no formal missionary emphasis. But throughout this time Robert Wilder and a group of twenty-one students were meeting regularly, in leisure hours or in the evenings, to pray that God would raise up from this conference a great host of missionary volunteers. One by one these students signed the Princeton Declaration stating that they were "desirous and willing, God permitting, to go to the unevangelized portions of the world."

On July 16, this group asked Dr. A. T. Pierson, editor of *The Missionary Review of the World* and a renowned Bible teacher, to address them on "God's Providence in Modern Missions." He "gave a thrilling address on missions. He supported, by convincing arguments, the striking proposition that 'all should go, and go to all.' This was a keynote which set many to thinking and praying."[4] As Hopkins says, "In this sermon Pierson expressed the germ of the idea that later crystallized as the watchword of the Student Volunteer Movement—'the evangelization of the world in this generation,' and was subsequently recognized as its originator."[5]

During the following week a great wave of missionary interest was building up. On July 24, these students persuaded Moody to let them hold a "meeting of the ten nations." They asked ten students representing ten different nations to address them on why they hoped to become foreign missionaries. Each one spoke for a few minutes to present the need of his area of the world and to appeal to the other students to volunteer for missionary service. Wishard and Dr. Pierson presided at the meeting, after which the students withdrew quietly to pray in their rooms or under the trees. Many more of them signed the Princeton Declaration, among them John R. Mott. Mott

---

[4] Mott, p. 4.
[5] Hopkins, p. 15.

later wrote that this meeting "may occupy as significant a place in the history of the Christian Church as the Williams Haystack Prayer Meeting."[6]

Through the remainder of the conference, these students continued to meet for prayer night after night. Before the closing night a total of ninety-nine had signed the Declaration. As they were gathered for their final session of prayer, one more young man slipped into the room to join them. Robert Wilder returned to Princeton with great joy to tell his sister Grace that their prayers had been answered.

The students were concerned lest the zeal of the summer conference should cool without spreading to other students who had not been able to attend. Thinking of the "Cambridge Seven" and their impact on fellow students, the students decided that a band of four young men should take the following school year to travel to as many campuses as possible. Their purpose would be to impart to others the same vision of God's mission to the world which they had received at Mt. Hermon. For a variety of reasons several were unable to fulfill their commitment on this, but it was finally agreed that Robert Wilder and another Princeton graduate, John Forman, should go. D. W. McWilliams, a Brooklyn layman, gladly underwrote the expenses of the tour.

During the school year of 1886-87, Wilder and Forman traveled to 162 institutions in the United States and Canada. Although hindered occasionally by poor health, they continued to pursue their goal. At times they traveled separately so as to reach as many campuses as possible. When separated, they kept in touch by almost daily post cards and by hourly prayer for each other. By the end of the year, they had seen 2,106 students sign the volunteer declaration, of whom about

---

[6] Mott, p. 4.

five hundred were women.[7] Among those who signed were Samuel Zwemer, who became the great apostle to the Muslims, and Robert E. Speer, destined to be one of the outstanding missionary statesmen of the next generation.

Upon the completion of their year of travels Forman sailed for India under the Presbyterian board, enjoying the generous financial support of his fellow Princeton students. There he served for thirty years in a distinguished career. Wilder, deciding to pursue further studies, entered Union Theological Seminary in New York in the fall of 1887. Thus the movement begun a year earlier was left virtually without direct leadership. The year of 1887-88 highlighted the need to consolidate what had been initiated at Mt. Hermon.

consolidation and organization

Wilder continued to give much attention to this movement by visiting churches and nearby colleges during his year of studies at Union. He was successful in helping another six hundred students decide to become foreign missionaries during that year. However, it was recognized that some form of organization would be necessary if they were not to lose the benefits of the uprising which had begun.

In July, 1888, fifty volunteers met again at Northfield, Massachusetts. They recognized certain danger signals already cropping up: the tendency to lose their unity, a tendency toward decline, a tendency to conflict with existing agencies.[8] Ober, McWilliams and others urged that some form of organization be drawn up.

The result was that an executive committee was formed with representatives from several cooperating movements.

[7] Wilder, p. 21.
[8] Mott, p. 6.

John R. Mott was chosen to represent the YMCA, Miss Nettie Dunn the YWCA and Robert Wilder the Inter-Seminary Missionary Alliance. Mott was unanimously chosen as chairman, and Wilder was named as traveling secretary.

On December 6, 1888, the movement was officially organized in New York City under the executive committee, taking the name of the Student Volunteer Movement for Foreign Missions. A fivefold purpose was developed:

The fivefold purpose of the Student Volunteer Movement is to lead students to a thorough consideration of the claims of foreign missions upon them personally as a lifework; to foster this purpose by guiding students who become volunteers in their study and activity for missions until they come under the immediate direction of the Mission Boards; to unite all volunteers in a common, organized, aggressive movement; to secure a sufficient number of well-qualified volunteers to meet the demands of the various Mission Boards; and to create and maintain an intelligent sympathetic and active interest in foreign missions on the part of students who are to remain at home in order to ensure the strong backing of the missionary enterprise by their advocacy, their gifts and their prayers.[9]

The slogan, "the evangelization of the world in this generation," became the great watchword of the SVM. This was misunderstood by some, notably Gustav Warneck, the German historian-theologian of mission, who thought it was an arrogant statement that all the world would be Christianized. It was branded as superficial and naive. However, Hogg has correctly placed it in perspective as follows:

---

[9] *Ibid.*, p. 8.

The majority of its detractors (most of them Continentals) apparently failed to grasp its true meaning. It did not prophesy nor suggest as possible the *conversion* of the world in this generation. . . . The overwhelming majority of students to whom it was meaningful understood by it the *responsibility* of each generation to make the gospel known to all mankind in that generation. None other can repeat that eternal message to a particular generation. Its own members alone can do that. Understanding this, individual Christians recognized more keenly than ever the bearing of the Great Commission upon their own lives. The watchword, then, in the best sense was a call to obligation—not a prophecy of fact.[10]

John R. Mott said later, "I can truthfully answer that next to the decision to take Christ as the Leader and Lord of my life, the watchword has had more influence than all other ideals and objectives combined to widen my horizon and enlarge my conception of the kingdom of God."[11]

Taking a cue from the Princeton Foreign Missionary Society with its "pledge," the SVM developed a declaration card. The purpose of the card was to face each student with the challenge of "the evangelization of the world in this generation." The card stated: "It is my purpose, if God permit, to become a foreign missionary." When a student signed this, it was understood as his response to the call of God. Every student was expected to face the issue and either to respond to it

---

[10] William Richey Hogg, *Ecumenical Foundations* (New York: Harper and Brothers, 1952), p. 88.

[11] *Christian Students and World Problems: Report on the Ninth International S.V.M. Convention, Indianapolis, 1924* (New York: Student Volunteer Movement), p. 64.

in the affirmative or else show that God was clearly leading him elsewhere.

growth and outreach

The growth of the SVM in the following three decades was nothing short of phenomenal. In 1891, the first international student missionary convention sponsored by SVM was held in Cleveland, Ohio. It was decided that such a convention should be held every four years in order to reach each student generation. Until the 1940's, this became a pattern, interrupted only by World War I. The first convention at Cleveland was attended by 558 students representing 151 educational institutions, along with 31 foreign missionaries and 32 representatives of missionary societies. [12]

By the time of the Cleveland convention, there were 6,200 Student Volunteers from 352 educational institutions in the United States and Canada. And 321 volunteers had already sailed for overseas service. In addition, 40 colleges and 32 seminaries were involved in financial support of their alumni who had gone overseas as Volunteers. [13] All of this had taken place in just five years since the Mt. Hermon conference. The Movement had also reached out and planted seeds of similar movements in Great Britain, Scandinavia and South Africa.

Luther Wishard's vision of a worldwide alliance of student movements such as the YMCA was bearing fruit in those same years. From 1888 to 1892, he traveled throughout the world "laying foundations for national Student Movements that were later to become members of the World's Student Christian Federation. Wishard was a Federation trailblazer. . . . John R.

---

[12] Wilder, p. 58.
[13] Omulogoli, p. 73.

Mott, however, did more than any other to found the World's Student Christian Federation."[14]

In 1895, at Vadstena Castle, Sweden, the World's Student Christian Federation was brought into being with John R. Mott as general secretary.[15] While the SVM was only one strand leading to the WSCF, it is notable that some of the leaders of the SVM were also leaders of the worldwide movement among students.

Following the meetings at Vadstena Castle, Mott spent the next two years traveling throughout the world. He visited universities in the Near East, India and Ceylon, China, Japan, Australia, New Zealand and Hawaii. Some seventy student associations and four national Student Christian Movements came into being as a result of his tour. "A world Christian statesman of abundant vigor and global vision was in the making."[16]

For the next twenty-five years, the story of the SVM is one of constant growth and outreach. An educational program in the schools was initiated and spread rapidly. Mott could later write that "At one time before the war the number in such circles exceeded 40,000 in 2,700 classes in 700 institutions."[17]

These efforts on the local campuses, the quadrennial conventions, plus literature, speaking tours and other activities resulted in thousands of students volunteering for overseas service. "By 1945, at the most conservative estimate, 20,500 students from so-called Christian lands, who had signed the

---

[14] Hogg, p. 89.

[15] See Ruth Rouse, *The World's Student Christian Federation: A History of the First Thirty Years* (London: S.C.M. Press, 1948).

[16] Hogg, p. 93.

[17] Mott, p. 12.

declaration, reached the field, for the most part under the missionary societies and boards of the Churches."[18]

World War I caused a temporary slowdown of these activities, but there was an immediate postwar burst of missionary zeal.

> The Convention held in Des Moines in 1920 marked the peak of the Movement's development. It was attended by 6,890 people from 949 schools and was followed by a peak year of newly enrolled Volunteers—2,783.[19]

The growth had been rapid and impressive. But SVM was now to experience the pressures of other forces that were building up in the aftermath of World War I. The "Roaring Twenties," the depression of the thirties and other currents did not leave SVM unscathed.

confusion and decline

Statistics can never give a full picture of any movement, any more than a thermometer can diagnose the disease of a patient. But just as a thermometer can give a reading on general health or decline, so statistics can often give readings of underlying symptoms of vigor or weakness. From the high point of 1920, the SVM experienced a rapid decline. Thirty-eight Volunteers sailed for the field in 1934 (as compared with 637 in 1921). Twenty-five Volunteers enrolled in SVM in 1938 (as compared with 2,783 in 1920). In 1940, 465 delegates attended the quadrennial convention in Toronto (as compared with the 6,890 at Des Moines in 1920). "These marks of the

---

[18]Ruth Rouse and Stephen C. Neill, *A History of the Ecumenical Movement, 1517-1948* (Philadelphia: Westminster Press, 1967), p. 328.

[19]William H. Beahm, *Factors in the Development of the Student Volunteer Movement for Foreign Missions*, unpublished Ph.D. dissertation, University of Chicago, 1941, p. 13.

Movement's decline were paralleled by internal strain, confusion and change."[20]

Here was a movement whose influence on students and the world mission of the church had been incalculable. Yet it could be said of SVM that "by 1940 it had almost ceased to be a decisive factor either in student religious life or in the promotion of the missionary program of the churches."[21]

What had happened to precipitate, or to allow, such a drastic decline?

Dr. Beahm has highlighted the following factors, while stating that no one reason by itself is an adequate explanation of the steady decline.

(1) Many changes of leadership broke the continuity of its life and left the subtle impression of a sinking ship from which they were fleeing.

(2) There was increasing difficulty in financing its program. This was closely related to the depression and the loss of Mott's leadership.

(3) The program tended to become top-heavy. In 1920 the Executive Committee was expanded from six to thirty members.

(4) Its emphasis upon foreign missions seemed to overlook the glaring needs in America, and so the Movement appeared to be specialized rather than comprehensive.

(5) When the interest of students veered away from missions, it left the Movement in a dilemma as to which interest to follow—student or missionary.

(6) There was a great decline in missionary education. One reason for this was the assumption that discussion of world problems by students was an improvement over the former

---

[20]*Ibid.*
[21]*Ibid.*, p. 4.

types of informative procedure. The Conventions came to have this discussional character.

(7) Their emphasis shifted away from Bible study, evangelism, lifework decision and foreign mission obligation on which the SVM had originally built. Instead they now emphasized new issues such as race relations, economic injustice and imperialism.

(8) The rise of indigenous leaders reduced the need for western personnel.

(9) The rise of the social gospel blotted out the sharp distinction between Christian America and the "unevangelized portions of the world."

(10) Revivalism had given way to basic uncertainty as to the validity of the Christian faith, especially of its claim to exclusive supremacy. Accordingly the watchword fell into disuse and the argument for foreign missions lost its force. [22]

The development of these trends is highlighted by the evaluations of the quadrennial conventions:

Des Moines, 1920

The convention at Des Moines in 1920 was a revolt against older leadership. The 5,000 students who gathered there were not dominated by any great missionary purpose. Many were not even professing Christians. They were more interested in peace relations, economic improvement, and international peace than in world evangelization as such. [23]

That convention was large in number but the delegates

---

[22]*Ibid.*, pp. 14-15.

[23]"Students and Missions at Buffalo," *The Missionary Review of the World,* XLV (February 1932), p. 67.

were lacking in missionary vision and purpose and were only convinced that a change of ideals and of leadership was needed. They rightly believed that selfishness and foolishness had involved the world in terrible war and bloodshed and they expressed their intention to take control of Church and State in an effort to bring about better conditions. The problems of international peace, social justice, racial equality and economic betterment obscured the Christian foundations and ideals of spiritual service. Many students were determined to work for reforms—either with or without the help of God.[24]

Indianapolis, 1924

The youth were in the saddle and turned attention from world evangelism to the solution of social and economic problems. But while earnest and energetic, they were uninformed and inexperienced. They failed to make much impression or to reach any practical conclusions. The SVM seemed doomed.[25]

Detroit, 1928

This convention seemed to offer a brief respite from the turbulence and upheavals of the two most recent ones. There was more of a quiet search for truth. Yet the uncertainty of belief on the part of many seemed to be evident.

The platform addresses were free from the impassioned oratory of the earlier Conventions; they were essentially a sharing of facts gleaned through experiences and observation. . . . Characteristic of the testimonies of foreigners

---

[24] "Student Volunteers at Indianapolis," *The Missionary Review of the World*, LIX (February 1936), p. 68.
[25] *Ibid.*

who spoke . . . was Hashim Hussein's on "A Moslem Meets Christ." . . . He referred to the numerous students at the conference whom he had observed were "talking in terms of comparative religion, of syncretism, and again students who (are) doubting one theological doctrine or another." . . . Beyond the Convention the mood of foreign missionary depression continued.[26]

Buffalo, 1932

The Buffalo Student Volunteer Convention was not exclusively a foreign missionary convention. The watchword of the movement—the Evangelization of the World in This Generation—was conspicuous by its absence.[27]

Indianapolis, 1936

The mass of the delegates had little or no knowledge of the Bible and spiritual things. They had evidently not studied the Bible in their homes, in churches or in colleges and universities. They lacked the background and foundations for the appreciation of missionary themes. . . . The audience was the mission field rather than the missionary force.[28]

In its fiftieth year of history, the character of the Movement had been so altered of late that it could not in all honesty claim to be contending for its originally outlined objectives. One clear indication of this fact is the place that was given the Movement's founder, Robert P. Wilder, in the programme of this Convention. . . . While

---

[26]Omulogoli, pp. 114-116.

[27]"Students and Missions at Buffalo," p. 67.

[28]"Student Volunteers at Indianapolis," p. 68.

many of the speakers held to philosophical and theological presuppositions that were not in accord with the Movement, Wilder was accorded no substantial role on the programme.[29]

termination of svm

As early as 1940, Dr. Beahm could write that the SVM "has almost ceased to be a decisive factor in the promotion of the missionary program of the churches." [30] After 1940, its activities appear to be almost nonexistent.

In 1959, the SVM merged with the United Student Christian Council and the Interseminary Movement to form the National Student Christian Federation (NSCF). This in turn was allied with the Roman Catholic National Newman Student Federation and other groups in 1966 to form the University Christian Movement (UCM). The purpose of the UCM at its inception was threefold: "to provide an ecumenical instrument for allowing the church and university world to speak to each other, to encourage Christian response on campuses to human issues, and to act as agent through which sponsors could provide resources and services to campus life." [31] It is obvious that these purposes, while legitimate in themselves, show little relationship to the original objectives of the SVM as spelled out at Mt. Hermon and in subsequent developments.

On March 1, 1969, the General Committee of the University Christian Movement at its meeting in Washington, D. C., took action in the form of an affirmative vote (23 for, 1 against, 1 abstention) on the following resolution: "We, the General Committee of the UCM, declare that as of June 30,

---

[29] Omulogoli, p. 121.

[30] Beahm, p. 16.

[31] Report of Religious News Service, April 1, 1969.

1969, the UCM ceases to exist as a national organization. . . ."[32]

Thus, the final vestiges of the greatest student missionary movement in the history of the church were quietly laid to rest eighty-three years after the Spirit of God had moved so unmistakably upon students at Mt. Hermon.

No human movement is perfect, nor can it be expected to endure indefinitely. But the great heritage left by the SVM can still speak to our generation. The reasons for its decline can serve as warning signals. Its principal emphases can redirect our attention to the basic issues of today: emphasis on personal commitment to Jesus Christ on a lifelong basis; acceptance of the authority of the Word of God and emphasis on personal Bible study; sense of responsibility to give the gospel of Christ to the entire world in our generation; reliance on the Holy Spirit; emphasis on student initiative and leadership to carry out these objectives.

---

[32] *News Notes*, Department of Higher Education, National Council of the Churches of Christ in the U.S.A., New York, XV, No. 3, March, 1969.

chapter 9

the student foreign missions fellowship

But Christian students were not to be deterred from fulfilling God's call. A growing concern was evident during the early 1930's that the church was somehow losing its vision of the world. The Great Depression was taking its toll economically in the church as elsewhere. The growing isolationism in international affairs was having its effect in a diminishing world outlook on the part of the church. In 1920, 1,731 missionaries sailed from North America for overseas service. By 1932, this number had dropped to 367.[1]

Unquestionably there were many factors that contributed to this drop, but there can be little doubt that the decrease in the influence of the SVM was an important one. Students were not blind to this, and many were uneasy about it. They saw the "establishment" (the government, social institutions, and the church) growing weaker in the confusion of the times. And

---

[1] Beahm, p. 13.

some students were determined to reverse the trend and rea-
waken the church to its worldwide responsibilities.

In June, 1936, fifty-three students from fourteen colleges
and Bible institutes, plus ten high schools, were gathered at
Ben Lippen Conference Center in Asheville, North Carolina.
During the week of June 15-22 they shared together, studying
the Word of God and discussing their responsibility to the
world. Great concern was expressed for the lack of missionary
emphasis on the campuses around the country.

The students consulted with Dr. Robert McQuilkin, founder and president of Columbia Bible College, whose total ministry was mission-oriented. Dr. McQuilkin had tried to go overseas as a missionary but had been hindered. When he founded
Columbia Bible College, he determined that it should be a
school where mission was a primary emphasis.[2] His Bible
teaching ministry, both at school and at conferences, invari-
ably showed the biblical basis of world outreach. The students
recognized in him a man of God who could encourage and
advise them on how to revive missionary interest in the colleges and Bible institutes of the day. In the spring of that same
year, Dr. McQuilkin had been used of God in a revival on the
campus of Wheaton College. One of the results of this was a
fresh awakening of missionary interest among the students.
Some of them were present at the Ben Lippen Conference.

Prayerful discussion of the problem resulted in forming a
small committee to consider starting a new movement that
would dedicate itself to the awakening of missionary interest
among students. The student chairman was Joseph
McCullough, who later became General Director of the Andes
Evangelical Mission. Two delegates were chosen to go to Kes-

---

[2] See Marguerite McQuilkin, *Always in Triumph* (Westwood, N.J.:
Revell, 1956).

wick, New Jersey, the following week where a similar student conference was to be held. On June 28-29, 1936, these delegates presented to the students at Keswick the burden God had placed upon them at Ben Lippen and enlisted their support.

Among those present at Keswick were several missionaries, including Miss Margaret Haines and Mrs. Harvey Borton, who had been Volunteers under SVM in former years. While they were grateful for all that SVM had meant in their own missionary career and while they longed to see SVM revived, they sympathized with the concern and vigor of these students. Realizing that the time had come for a new approach, they joined in encouraging them to move ahead with their plans.

As had happened at Mt. Hermon exactly fifty years earlier, these students laid the groundwork for a movement that was soon to touch the lives of thousands of students on behalf of overseas missions. It was agreed that the new movement should be called the Student Foreign Missions Fellowship.[3] Upon returning to their respective campuses, they began immediately to form local chapters of SFMF. Prayer bands, Bible study groups, chapter meetings and other activities were utilized to bring before the student body the claims of God upon his church for a worldwide outreach. The first two years of initial growth were under a loosely-knit form of organization. Wilbert Norton, who had been present at Ben Lippen in 1936, served as part-time national secretary. (Dr. Norton subsequently went to Africa as a missionary and later became Professor of Missions at Wheaton College Graduate School of Theology.)

---

[3] Data on SFMF is drawn from the files in the national headquarters of IVCF, from personal interviews and from the author's own involvement in the movement.

In December, 1938, a constitutional convention was held at Keswick, New Jersey, with sixty delegates from seventeen schools in attendance. Dr. Thomas Lambie, missionary to Palestine, and Dr. McQuilkin were invited as speakers. A constitution and doctrinal statement were adopted. An executive committee composed of students and other Christian leaders was chosen to direct the work. National student officers were elected.

The first full-time general secretary for SFMF, Kenneth Hood, was named at that time. (Dr. Hood has subsequently worked for many years in Costa Rica.) Between 1936 and 1945 (when the merger with IVCF was effected), SFMF had a total of seven part- or full-time secretaries, each of whom served for only a year or two at most. Such a rapid turnover occurred because every one of them moved out quickly into missionary service in other parts of the world.[4]

In 1940, a publication entitled "News *F*rom *M*ission *F*ronts" (utilizing the initials FMF) was started with the purpose of circulating missionary news to the campuses.

It is significant that all of this was going on during the depression of the thirties when most mission boards were curtailing their activities and in many cases retreating from advance bases. The students' unswerving faith that God could and would supply their needs was honored by God.

Taking a cue from the SVM they developed a missionary

---

[4] National secretaries of SFMF and missionary directors of IVCF/ SFMF have been: Joseph McCullough (1936-1937), Wilbert Norton (1937-1938), Kenneth Hood (1939), Neill Hawkins (1940-1941), Peter Stam, III (1942-1943), Herbert Anderson (1944-1945), Christy Wilson, Jr. (1946-1947), T. Norton Sterret (1947-1948), Wesley Gustafson (1949-1952), David Adeney (1953-1956), Eric Fife (1958-1968), David Howard (1969-).

decision card which stated:

Knowing that Jesus Christ has saved me from my sin; that all men without Christ are lost, and there is no other name by which men may be saved; that God's command is, "Go ye into all the world"; that the laborers are few in the foreign field; and believing it is God's will for me, *I purpose to be a foreign missionary*, and will plan accordingly. Until He leads me to the field, I will support the work by my prayers, gifts, and witnessing. If the Lord's later leading should direct me into other service, I will seek to give foreign missions its rightful place of prominence in my ministry.

Summer deputation teams of students became a part of the movement. The first team traveled in 1938. In the summer of 1941, a team of students traveled thirteen thousand miles through twenty states of the middle west and Pacific coast, conducting 115 services. During this trip they saw 224 young people sign missionary decision cards.

By October, 1941, there were thirty-six chapters of SFMF with 2,628 members in different parts of the country.

In 1939, the Inter-Varsity Christian Fellowship moved into the United States from Canada. The threefold purpose of IVCF was: (1) to witness to the Lord Jesus Christ as God Incarnate, and to seek to lead others to personal faith in him as Lord and Savior, (2) to deepen and strengthen the spiritual life of students by the study of the Bible, by prayer, and by Christian Fellowship, and (3) to present the call of God to the foreign mission field and so help all students to discover God's role for them, at home or abroad, in worldwide evangelization.

Since this third purpose of IVCF overlapped directly with the purposes of SFMF, it was not long before talks of cooperation began to develop. Careful study was given for several years to the possibilities and implications of a merger. When both groups were satisfied that a merger could help them to fulfill more effectively their mission from God on the campuses, it was formally consummated in November, 1945. The SFMF now became the missionary arm of the IVCF. Since that time SFMF has concentrated primarily on the campuses of Christian schools (Bible institutes, theological seminaries and Christian liberal arts colleges), while IVCF works primarily on the secular campuses.

From September, 1945, to January, 1946, during the period when the merger was being effected, Wilbert Norton, home on furlough from his first term in Africa, was asked to serve as interim SFMF secretary. He held the reins until J. Christy Wilson, Jr., first IVCF Missionary Secretary, could take over.

The Missionary Secretary of IVCF served also as director of the SFMF. On the campuses of the secular colleges and universities where IVCF was active, his responsibilities were to help Christian students consider God's claims on their lives in terms of the needs of the world as a whole. Every IVCF staff member was expected to help students include the third purpose of the movement in their own personal thinking as well as in their programs. On the campuses of Christian schools where SFMF was active, the Missionary Secretary served in a similar way but in the context of a campus where the majority of the students had already made a commitment to Christ.

The impact of the SVM quadrennial conventions was clearly evident to the leaders of SFMF. From the beginning of the movement they planned an annual student missionary convention. During World War II this was reduced to a biennial convention. Following the merger with IVCF, plans were made, under Christy Wilson, Jr., to expand this into a continent-wide biennial convention that would be far larger in scope and could make an impact on the entire Christian student world and on the church at large.

The first IVCF-SFMF international student missionary convention was held at the University of Toronto during the Christmas vacation of 1946. Five hundred seventy-five students from 151 schools attended. In 1948, the convention was moved to the University of Illinois at Urbana, where it has been held every three years since that time. It has come to be known commonly as "the Urbana Convention." In 1967, over nine thousand students and missionaries attended the eighth convention. This was probably the largest student missionary gathering ever held.

The purpose of the Urbana conventions have been three-fold: (1) to lay a biblical foundation through scriptural exegesis for the world mission of the church, (2) to bring students into contact with the world situation by letting them face the issues of the day and interact with Christian leaders from around the world, and (3) to relate these two factors to each student in such a way that he can respond intelligently to God's demands upon his life in seeking where God wishes to use him.

The convention has never shied away from the burning issues of the day. In plenary sessions, in elective workshops, in forums, in question panels and in other ways vital topics are discussed. These have included such things as missions and the race issue, social concern, paternalism, colonialism, missions and the national church, communism and similar topics. Students are made aware of the varieties of service available to them overseas and the different methods of missionary work being used. Modern communications (radio, television, cinema), aviation, literature, medicine, the performing arts, student evangelism, church planting, discipleship training, education—these are just a few.

Missions are thus set in the context of the actual world of

the day. The tension between Western Christianity and other cultures is faced and discussed openly. Students are encouraged to interact personally with the speakers and the many missionary representatives who are present.

In 1967, the convention theme—"God's Men: From All Nations To All Nations"—highlighted the fact that IVCF does not believe that North America is the only sending area of the world. Rather, as Christians we are part of the worldwide body of Christ. The responsibility for world evangelism rests upon all Christians throughout the world. Today hundreds of missionaries around the world will testify that God first spoke to them about overseas service at Urbana.

Following World War II, there was a great upsurge in missionary interest throughout the church and the student world. Veterans of the war had returned to the college campuses to complete their education. They had been around the world and had seen the spiritual and social needs of their fellowman in Europe and the Orient. They had faced death and were sobered about the values of life. General MacArthur was calling for ten thousand missionaries to go to Japan. Similar calls were coming from other parts of the world. The rise in missionary volunteers was dramatic.

World War II veterans were joining together in forming new missionary societies to help meet the needs they had seen overseas and to utilize the training they had received in the military service. Such groups as Missionary Aviation Fellowship, Far Eastern Gospel Crusade and Greater Europe Mission were founded primarily by these men.

SFMF rode the wave of missionary enthusiasm. Chapters grew in strength and influence. In many schools the SFMF chapter became the largest student organization on the campus. At Wheaton College with fifteen hundred students, for example, attendance at weekly SFMF meetings often averaged three to five hundred, and special events would attract up to eight hundred. This chapter was led by Jim Elliot as president, who was later to die as a martyr among the Auca Indians of Ecuador in 1956. His influence on the campus as an outstanding scholar (graduated with highest honor), athlete (champion wrestler) and all-around spiritual leader was incalculable. More students went from that campus to the mission field during this period than in any other period in the history of the college.

SFMF profited by the mature leadership given by war veterans whose age, experience and vision of the world provided a strong foundation for campus activities. The names of some of today's outstanding missionary leaders around the world can be found on the rosters of SFMF chapters of those years.

During the decade of the 1950's (sometimes referred to as "The Silent Fifties"), there was a period of settling down on campuses. It was a time of "catching our breath" after the furious decades of the first half of the twentieth century. World War I, the Roaring Twenties, the Great Depression of the thirties, World War II and its aftermath in the forties seemed to leave the human race begging for a breather. People in general, including the students, seemed to appreciate a chance to live a quieter life without the pressures of causes. The activism of the sixties had not yet arisen.

The general lull in the atmosphere took its toll on the church and its evangelistic outreach. This was reflected also among students in a lessening of missionary interest. SFMF began to feel the effects. As there was less interest in campus activities of many sorts, there was less interest in the outreach of SFMF. Statistically SFMF declined somewhat during the fifties. In 1951, the national office was in contact with 3,082 students who had signed missionary decision cards. In 1954, this figure was 2,278 and in 1958, it was 2,647. The word "apathy" was being used with increasing frequency to describe student attitudes.

Then came the sixties. They started off with a new surge of rising hopes. Youth became a new factor in national life. As never before students began to make their voice heard. No politician, no industry, no movement which hoped to make progress dared to ignore the impact that youth was making on society. Unfortunately, before the decade was over many of the hopes and aspirations had been dashed in bitter disillusionment. While it is beyond the scope of this book to discuss the implications of that decade, it must be stated that the revitalization of students as a major factor in national life also had its effect within the SFMF.

In the early 1960's, students in the southeastern region of the United States became concerned over the condition of SFMF not only on the local campuses of Christian schools but also on the national level. Paul Bowers, grandson of Dr. Robert McQuilkin, took a major lead in this at Columbia Bible College.

The students expressed a concern to revitalize the organization that God had raised up in the past. They did not seek change for the sake of change. There was no desire just to break with the past. At the same time they were convinced that merely preserving "the good old days" was inadequate. Renewed life and imaginative outreach to correspond with the changing times was needed.

The national office of SFMF had been unable to give adequate personal supervision and counsel to the many chapters spread across the country. This led understandably to a feeling of disillusionment on the part of some students who wondered if the national office was really interested in them. On the other hand, shortage of personnel and finances made it impossible for the missionary director to have as much direct contact with local groups as he would have liked.

In 1962 and 1964, several informal meetings were held by students from Columbia Bible College, Wheaton College and Moody Bible Institute to study what could be done to inject new life into the SFMF. For a while it appeared that a new movement, separate from SFMF, was in the making.

At the seventh IVCF Missionary Convention at Urbana in December, 1964, concerned students from a number of Christian schools met with Eric Fife, Missionary Director of IVCF, to discuss revitalizing the SFMF. A committee of students, called the Inter-regional Coordinating Committee (ICC), was appointed. Its purposes were to reopen communications among the SFMF chapters and help to coordinate activities of SFMF in regional groupings in the southeast, northeast and midwest.

In 1965, IVCF appointed Evan Adams as Assistant Missionary Director with primary responsibility for working with SFMF groups. Rapport between the students and the national office improved as Mr. Adams was able to spend more time with them personally in campus visits. A new monthly news bulletin reported what was being done on different campuses and how the missionary emphasis could be improved.

During the next three years, Mr. Fife and Mr. Adams met with student leaders to discuss long-range policies and campus strategy of SFMF and the ICC. Student initiative was the major factor in this planning. An Advisory Committee for SFMF was set up. It was composed of student leaders, IVCF representatives and mission board representatives. Old suspicions began to evaporate as communications improved.

The students cooperated with Mr. Adams in planning the first annual leadership training workshop for members of SFMF chapters in June, 1967. While attendance was low, it grew in subsequent years. The workshop has now become a vital and significant part of the movement, with students carrying increasing responsibility in the planning and execution. Leaders of the ICC also began visiting other campuses to stimulate renewed missionary interest. They set goals for themselves to establish vital SFMF groups on certain campuses within specific periods of time. A new sense of unity and forward vision became evident.

Another significant result of this student initiative was the effect it had on mission boards. The Evangelical Foreign Missions Association (EFMA) and the Interdenominational Foreign Missions Association (IFMA), which between them represented approximately 113 mission boards, both named Personnel and Student Affairs Commissions.[5] Their purpose was to keep lines of communications open with the students, to learn from them, to help them wherever possible and in general to cooperate in a reawakening of missionary interest among students. Student representatives were invited on several occasions to their national conventions to share student viewpoints on missions.

Once again, as he had done so often in the past, God was laying his hand on students as his instrument to revive missionary interest.

[5] *North American Protestant Ministries Overseas*, 8th ed. (Waco, Texas: Word Books, 1968).

PART III: THE CONTEMPORARY PERSPECTIVE

chapter 10

critical, restless, honest, concerned

What has God said? What has God done? What does God want to do?

These questions can be asked legitimately in relation to God's plan for the world mission of the church. In the first part, The Biblical Perspective, I have tried to summarize what God has said about the responsibility of the church in world outreach. Part II, The Historical Perspective, has given a view of what God has done through students in influencing the church to fulfill those obligations. It now remains to ask what God wants to do through students today.

the past generations and missions

The divine mandate is clear. It begins in Genesis 1 and is present throughout the entire Scriptures. God's concern is worldwide. How the church has responded to that mandate is also clear in the light of history. All too frequently the church has fallen into lethargy in relation to its worldwide obligations. But God does not leave himself without a witness. Whether it be a Nicolas von Zinzendorf, a Samuel J. Mills, a C. T. Studd, a Robert Wilder, a John R. Mott, a Jim Elliot or a hundred others who could be named, God singles out a man to prophesy to his church. *And with remarkable frequency that man has been a student*!

If this is true (and history confirms that it is), is it too much to believe that God, whose commands have not been withdrawn, may choose again to move upon the church through students?

Looking at history for a moment from the purely human viewpoint, one could ask, Would the Society of Brethren with its lasting influence for world outreach ever have been born but for the students who prayed under a haystack? Would the first overseas mission board in North America have come into existence but for the concern of Samuel J. Mills and his colleagues? Would the Student Volunteer Movement have stimulated the sending of over twenty thousand missionaries had it not been for students who prayed at Mt. Hermon? Would the Student Foreign Missions Fellowship of IVCF have taken up the cause of world missions apart from students who prayed at Ben Lippen and Keswick? Or would the SFMF have survived the apathy of later years without the concern of students who refused to close their ears to God's commands and the world situation?

the now generation and missions

Perhaps no previous generation has been so dissected, analyzed, synthesized and categorized as this one. The influence of students on the life of the nation has become one of the major factors of our time. Sociologists, historians, educators, theologians, politicians, business men and others will be debating this influence for years to come. This is not the place for a full scale discussion of the characteristics of students today. But it is certainly fitting to ask how the "Now Generation" will relate to the world mission of the church in the light of the biblical commands and the rich heritage of the past.

Students today are *more critical* than ever before. The advance of science and technology has placed at the disposal of the educational community tools and methods for acquiring and analyzing knowledge which are far more sophisticated than anything known before. Consequently, students have more techniques available for critical examination of the world.

And this can be positive. In the area of missions a critical nature can be quite valuable. Many of the greatest pioneers of world outreach in other eras were critical men. William Carey was critical of the church in England in the 1790's for its failure to reach out to the world. His criticism forced the church to look beyond its own borders and to send him to India. Samuel J. Mills was, to a degree, critical of the failure of the church of his day in North America, and his concern resulted in the many activities already related. Hudson Taylor, upon arriving in China, was critical of the missions that worked only on the coast and neglected the vast interior of that country with its hundreds of millions of people. So he founded the China Inland Mission to witness to those not being reached by others.

Had these men not been critical in a positive sense, who knows what the era of modern missions would have been? If today's students can channel their criticism to creative and progressive ideas for world outreach with the gospel and not just to the destruction of outmoded patterns or institutions, then the church could well witness another great forward movement toward the completion of the Great Commission.

Who could deny that students today are *restless* and *impatient*? Man with his advanced technology set foot on the moon, and we sat in our living rooms and watched the event unfold before our eyes. So students ask, If we can do this, why can't we solve the problems of mankind that surround us every day here on earth? "Peace *now!*" is a universal student cry.

Restlessness, too, can be positive. Did not God call Abraham to mobility? Did he not make clear to his people that "here we have no continuing city, but we seek one to come"? Did not the Apostle Paul find it impossible to rest in any one place, always striving to "preach the gospel not where Christ has already been named," or "in lands beyond you"? The spirit that moved students to cry, "The evangelization of the world in this generation," was a restless spirit. The urgency of the task of world evangelism can be greatly enhanced if today's restless students come to sense the impatience of God himself to bring men around the world to Jesus Christ.

Students today are constantly emphasizing a *genuine concern for human values.* Is all this talk just a put on? Anyone who thinks so reveals his gross ignorance of the depth of compassion students feel for their fellow man. Participation in Headstart teaching, in poverty programs, in inner city projects, in ecological concerns, in hunger marches to raise money which will not benefit them personally, in Peace Corps work with low pay and sometimes meager tangible results—all demonstrate a desire to serve mankind.

Such concerns, when applied to world evangelism, could give the church a renewed and much needed emphasis on the needs of man in his totality. All too often a false dichotomy has arisen between the physical and spiritual needs of man.

In its concern for man's physical needs, the social gospel of an earlier generation lost sight of the spiritual side (and thus of the primacy of evangelism). The evangelical church, in its reaction to that extreme, has sometimes lost sight of the great exhortations of Scripture to see man as a total being with physical as well as spiritual needs.

Students today not only react against the materialism so prevalent in our affluent society, but they also are expressing a positive concern for human values. Happily churches in many parts of the world are also reawakening to this angle of evangelism. The biblical altruism of students can now find a legitimate outlet for service in world evangelism. And students' rejection of affluence enhances their ability to be mobile.

What of today's students' desire for *honesty*? "Tell it like it is" (already a cliche) seems to typify the demand for sincerity. Students want openness from peers as well as from elders and are ready to give the same. Hypocrisy of any sort is looked upon as one of the gravest sins.

Students feel that mission representatives have tended to tell only what they think the church at home wants to hear, thus giving a distorted picture of life as it really is. But students will respond to the missionary who will share in all honesty the failures, defeats, tragedies and incomprehensible elements as well as the triumphs of missionary life. Is this not a healthy thing for all concerned? Can a church or a mission rightfully complain if it is forced into a re-evaluation of its honesty?

Summing up why students are being called the "Now Generation," Dr. Seymour L. Halleck, professor of psychiatry at the University of Wisconsin, says:

Students today have little reverence for the past and little hope for the future. They are trying to live in the present. The most important reason for this is the ever-increasing rate of change which characterizes our society. When no one can predict what the world will be like in 20, 10 or even 5 years, man must alter his psychological perspectives. The lessons of the past become less relevant; planning for the future appears futile. One is driven to gear his value system towards enjoyment of the present. . . . Youth are no lazier, no more hedonistic or passive than their parents. Rather, conditions do not favor future-oriented values, and youth are being forced into the role of the "now generation."[1]

the now generation and images of missions

How does this generation of students view the missionary enterprise of the church? It is not surprising that students who are critical, restless, concerned for human values and honest would have some decided ideas about missions. Certain words which used to carry an aura of positive content now tend to bring forth a negative reaction. Words such as "missionary" and "foreign missions" are prime examples.

Here are a few of the images which are conjured up in the minds of students when the word "missionary" is mentioned: *spinster, fink, outmoded, cannibal, dowdy, old-fashioned, slides, poor dress, no makeup, jungle, dirty word, ridiculous, poor, dumb, bore, zop, old fogey, tiger, haggard, talker, nut, glasses, savage, prejudiced, stupid, harmful.* Lest anyone think that this list has been exaggerated or fabricated, it was taken verbatim from responses given by committed Christian students from a wide variety of schools, both Christian and secular.

Two things need to be said about these reactions. First, to missionaries. If this is the idea that students have of missionaries (whether or not it is correct), then a lot of self-examination is called for. If missionaries have given some justification for such ideas, serious re-evaluation is in order. Even if the reactions should be unfair or incorrect, a vast area of re-educa-

---

[1] Seymour L. Halleck, "Why They'd Rather Do Their Own Thing," *Think,* September-October, 1968, p. 3.

tion is necessary to open lines of communications again.

Second, to students. Even if these ideas were 100 percent correct when applied to every missionary in the world (and even the most vehement opponent of missions would scarcely be prepared to maintain that), the question must be asked, *"What has this got to do with my obedience to God?"* The biblical mandates for world evangelism as given by God throughout the Bible and as underscored by Christ cannot be avoided. Just because I may react negatively to those who have responded to that mandate is no excuse for my ignoring God's commands to me.

Our man-made images of missions and the eternal, unchangeable commands of God are two vitally different things and must not be confused.

In order to set this in the proper perspective it should be noted that students who attended the Eighth Inter-Varsity Missionary Convention at Urbana, Illinois, in 1967, came away with a high view of missions and missionaries. In response to a questionnaire used after the convention, students revealed some valuable insights.

When asked, "What words do you associate with missions?" many checked words with a positive overtone.[2] The sociologists analyzing the response commented, "There is a general sense of the servant role. The 'great commission' is still foremost in the minds of many. Missions are viewed as 'challenging.' "[3] Furthermore, they write, "Only slightly more than

---

[2] Of course, since this survey was taken after the students had met a number of personable missionaries, their favorable response is not surprising.

[3] Barkman, Dayton, and Gruman, *Christian Collegians and Foreign Missions* (Monrovia, California: Missions Advanced Research and Communications Center, 1969), p. 60.

20% are willing to write off missions, as they are presently conducted, as not being effective."[4]

When asked about "the really important reason (or reasons) for conducting foreign missionary activity," the response was encouraging.

A significant number (35%) are not willing to see the condition of men as the important reason for missions, but rather taking action on God's command.[5]

The vast majority of the delegates to Urbana believe that every Christian has some kind of obligation to missions, even though every Christian is not called to be an overseas missionary.[6]

This indicates a genuine concern for missions, motivated by obedience to God rather than by concern for men alone.

the now generation and history

History can be either a prison or a pedestal: a prison to bind us to the past or a pedestal from which to view the future and launch out to new horizons. If history is allowed to be a prison, it becomes the enemy of progress. "The good old days" cannot be revived, and it is no use for an older generation to lament their passing. Besides, every generation will have its "good old days" to look back upon when they have advanced with the years.

On the other hand, if history is ignored, then the old dictum comes into play: "Those who refuse to learn from history are condemned to repeat it." Voices from the past can spell out the dangers and pitfalls into which other generations fell.

---

[4] *Ibid.*, p. 72.

[5] *Ibid.*, p. 30.

[6] *Ibid.*, p. 66.

To avoid those same mistakes, one must know what they were and why they were committed.

Any generation that desires true progress must stand on the shoulders of its forebears. It can be grateful for the heritage they have left in positive ways. It can learn from their failures and determine not to be caught in the same mistakes.

In the post World War I era, the prevailing atmosphere of the times caused students to abandon the original purposes of the Student Volunteer Movement (evangelism, Bible study, lifework decision and foreign missions). Active involvement in the social issues of the day was, hopefully, to usher in a new world which would be free from war, greed and hatred. The cries of the immediate drowned out the call of the future, and overseas missions were neglected.

While the social problems that had to be faced were gigantic, the failure came partly in making it an "either-or" situation. It was either foreign missions or social issues, not "both-and." The "either-or" course of action led to the collapse of student influence for world evangelism. But it also led to the collapse of the movement in general. It was not long before SVM was neither a force for missions nor for social change.

the now generation and now

Today we stand at a similar juncture in history. There is strong pressure from some quarters to abandon emphasis on world outreach in favor of more attention to the social issues on our doorstep. These problems are urgent and demand our attention and action. We dare not ignore them. To do so would be to reject the Word of God which speaks clearly to such issues: "If a brother or sister is ill-clad and in lack of daily food, and one of you says to them, 'Go in peace, be warmed and filled,' without giving them the things needed for the body, what does it profit? So faith by itself, if it has no works, is dead" (Jas.

2:15-17).

At the same time the commands of Jesus Christ for world evangelism are unequivocal. They have not yet been fulfilled. Therefore, they still stand. It is not within our rights to question or ignore them. We are to obey them.

But let us not fall into the error of "either-or." God's call to his church is a call to serve the total needs of man: physical, intellectual, emotional and spiritual. It is a grave misconception to imagine so-called missionary work as being just "spiritual." A true missionary sees man as an integrated whole and goes to him with the redeeming message of Jesus Christ who will meet all of his needs.

It is equally erroneous to imagine that the person interested in the burning social issues of the day will find fulfillment only in working in North America. If ghettos are a problem here (and they are), what of the ghettos of Calcutta, Bombay, Hong Kong, Lima or Caracas? The urban slums of Africa, Asia and Latin America present problems which in depth and scope match or surpass any we know in North America.

Consider the lonely peasant who has been lured to the big city by the promise of "El Dorado," only to be hopelessly swallowed up in a way of life which he cannot comprehend and in which he cannot earn a living. The already overcrowded slums, where starvation reigns as king, suck him inexorably into their orbit. Once caught in the vicious circle of poverty, exploitation and cultural confusion, his only recourse is to see how long he can stave off final starvation. Digging in the garbage cans and refuse heaps of the city is often the only possible alternative for a man who retains enough self-dignity not to beg.

But few can fend off the ogre-like pressures of begging. And when this becomes intolerable, robbery offers a supposedly easier way of subsistence. A hovel slapped together out of cardboard, tin barrels and bamboo poles, covered with a roof of palm branches or tar paper, is probably his home. The underside of a bridge offers an attractive spot to build, as the material for a roof and one wall is already there.

If the church is to speak and act in the realm of poverty and ghettos, by what process of reasoning do we conclude that this must automatically be limited to the United States?

Or consider the racial issue. No one can deny that this rates top priority in North America as a problem to be solved. But somehow we have been led to believe that it exists only in the United States and South Africa. Nothing could be further from the truth. Unquestionably it has come to the surface more here than anywhere else. It has been analyzed, debated and fought over with more overt violence here than in any other part of the world. But it is a grave misconception to assume that it does not exist elsewhere. Listen, for example, to this actual conversation between a Latin American and a North American. It took place on a bus in Colombia.

"How is it that you North Americans permit all the racial discimination which exists in your country? How can you tolerate such inequality?"

"I don't defend that. I consider it one of the greatest evils we know today, and it is a black mark on my country. But let me ask you one question, Do you not have any segregation in this country?"

"Of course not! You never saw a segregated school or bus here. We're all equal, regardless of color."

"Permit me one more question. Did you ever see a black army officer here?"

"*What*! A black man giving orders!"

In another Latin American country a local exclusive club wanted to offer guest membership to a visiting group of foreign dignitaries during their stay in the country. But when they discovered that some of the foreigners were black, the owners of the club were thrown into an intolerable dilemma. No black had ever entered the club before, and the club was not prepared to make a change now.

Or consider a national friend of mine overseas who wanted to enroll his son in a good school for advanced education. When asked why he didn't choose a certain school recommended to him, his fatalistic reply was, "His skin is too dark to be accepted there."

The racial issue is definitely not limited to North America. It is far more worldwide than is usually admitted. Few and far between have been the articles or books which discuss openly and frankly the racial issue in any country other than the United States or South Africa. But the truth is something quite different. Anyone who wants to help alleviate this cancerous sore from the human race will find all the challenge he needs in scores of other countries.

Or what of ecology? Is the United States the only country which is failing to conserve its natural resources or to control its environment?

A few years ago I made my first visit to a tiny village in Colombia called Corozalito. It was nestled deep in the lush jungles and tropical rain forests. The last time I went to that village (only a few years later), I walked for miles across open plains, with no jungle in sight. The land had been razed and burned for farming purposes, stripping it of all natural protection. Water had become scarce, and an arid surrounding was the predominant effect. One farmer lamented that two of his streams had practically disappeared. All efforts to explain the relation of trees to water had so far fallen on deaf ears.

Water pollution is a major problem in the United States. But anyone who has traveled in rural areas elsewhere in the world has probably suffered personally from the effects of

water pollution. The agonies of dysentery and intestinal para-
sites can only be appreciated by those who have experienced
them. I have been in situations overseas where my only water
supply was covered with green scum and polluted by nearby
human and animal refuse. This sort of problem has terrifying
effects on the children and thus on future generations of the
population.

Any young person today who wishes to combine a concern
for the earth which God has given us with a desire to share the
gospel of Christ will find more than he can handle in the
developing countries of the Third World. To be sure, ecological
problems are not an exclusive North American monopoly.

In other words, responding to God's call to serve in an area
other than North America by no means excludes the possibility of becoming involved in the issues of the day. On the
contrary, *it more likely will increase that possibility many
times over*. Some of the most effective gospel preaching today
is going on where it is being combined with a concern for the
physical and environmental needs of the people to whom the
message is given.

On the walls of the Stanford Memorial Church at Stanford
University, California, is the following quotation:

There is no narrowing so deadly as the narrowing of
man's horizons of spiritual things. No worse evil could
befall him in his course on earth than to lose sight of
heaven.

In our preoccupation with the urgent temporal needs around
us are we in danger of narrowing our horizons, both spiritual
and geographical? Are we looking only at the needs we can see
and neglecting those which we cannot see but which may be
just as great? Are we looking only at the physical and social
needs which are so evident around us and failing to see similar
needs elsewhere in the world? Have we allowed an "either-or"

situation to develop in our thinking and thus mistakenly differentiated between spiritual and social, our country and overseas?

Jesus Christ said, "I came that they may have life, and have it abundantly. I am the good shepherd. . . . And I have other sheep, that are not of this fold; I must bring them also, and they will heed my voice. So there shall be one flock, one shepherd."

appendix

some observations on the charismatic movement*

During the recent growth of the church in Latin America, a problem arose regarding the gift of tongues. During this time I drew up a paper to provide some guidelines for the Latin American Mission. While not an official declaration of Mission policy, it outlined what we believe the Scriptures teach and what our responsibility should be in helping the churches. It has since been found useful to a wider audience.

After an introductory statement on the charismatic movement, the paper continued:

In view of this situation we wish to state as clearly as possible our understanding of the teaching of the Word of God on such matters and how we strive to apply these teachings in our ministry.

---

*This appendix has been previously published in *Hammered As Gold* and is reprinted here by permission of Harper and Row.

I. The Bible is the Word of God in its entirety and its truths must be ministered in the power of the Holy Spirit.

Christ warned the Sadducees, "Ye do err, not knowing the Scriptures, nor the power of God" (Matt. 22:29). While Christ was speaking of a specific doctrinal issue here, He was certainly enunciating a basic principle, namely, the tension or balance between the written Word of God in its doctrinal presentation and the power of the Spirit of God in applying that Word. These two factors must always be kept paramount in our ministry: *the Word of God* as the basis for all our work and teachings, and *the power of God* in our lives as we minister His Word to others. The Word of God without His accompanying power in our lives becomes ineffective; the power of God in our experience, unless grounded in the Word of God, may be misunderstood and thus lead into error. We seek a holy combination of God's Word enacted in power in our daily lives and ministry by His Spirit.

II. The continual infilling of the Holy Spirit is indispensable to an effective ministry of the Word of God.

We wish to be open to whatever the fullness of the Spirit may mean for us. We recognize that the Spirit of God may choose, in His sovereignty, to work in ways which we may not have anticipated but which will always be in accord with the clear teachings of God's Word.

This happened to the Apostle Peter in Acts 10 in the case of Cornelius. Peter's understanding of the Scriptures was incomplete at that time, and he was forced to re-evaluate his interpretations in the light of what God wanted to do for the Gentiles. It was *the power of God* coming upon Cornelius and his household that forced Peter to recognize his own deficiency in understanding *the Word of God*. God's Word had not changed, but Peter's understanding of it had.

We seek before God to preach and teach His Word as He enables us to understand it. If, in the course of our ministry, the Holy Spirit chooses to do unexpected things, we accept this as the power of God, which will always be manifested in accord with the Word of God.

The Bible exhorts us to "be filled with the Spirit" (Eph. 5:18). This will come in harmony with and through the application of God's Word. When this fullness is accompanied by gifts of the Spirit, we rejoice with all those who are blessed by such gifts and accept them as part of God's plan for the edification of the Body of Christ.

We purpose, therefore, with God's help to "follow after . . . reaching forth unto those things which are before, . . . press toward the mark for the prize of the high calling of God in Christ Jesus" (Phil. 3:12-14). Then we can say with Paul, "And if in any thing ye be otherwise minded, God shall reveal even this unto you" (Phil. 3:15). Thus, if God wishes to reveal Himself afresh through His power, in accord with His unchangeable Word, we stand ready to admit our own limited understandings and to receive any new infilling which He wants to give us.

III. Openness to the true work of the Holy Spirit must be accompanied by a diligent effort to guard against errors and excesses, false teachings and practices:

This statement requires an amplification in the following terms:

1. We believe that the gifts of the Spirit enumerated in Romans 12, I Corinthians 12, and Ephesians 4 may be apportioned to every man as the Spirit wills. If the Spirit chooses to manifest any or all of these gifts in our day, we accept this as part of His sovereign plan for the church.

2. At the same time we do not believe that every outward

manifestation of a so-called "gift" is necessarily from the Spirit of God. On the contrary the Bible teaches that the opposite is true. "Many will say to me in that day, Lord, Lord, have we not prophesied in thy name? and in thy name have cast out devils? and in thy name done many wonderful works? And then will I profess unto them, I never knew you; depart from me, ye that work iniquity" (Matt. 7:22, 23). "For there shall arise false Christs, and false prophets, and shall show great signs and wonders; insomuch that, if it were possible, they shall deceive the very elect" (Matt. 24:24). Thus the Devil may counterfeit the gifts of the Spirit, and this requires constant vigilance on our part, warning and instructing our brethren against such errors.

3. No single gift of the Spirit is the indispensable sign of the fullness of the Spirit. Some teach earnestly that speaking in tongues will accompany the true fullness or baptism of the Holy Spirit. We believe the Bible teaches that tongues are given to some for edification (I Cor. 14:4, 5) but not to all (I Cor. 12:10, 30). Whether tongues be viewed as a gift or a sign, or both, the Bible nowhere teaches that all believers must experience this phenomenon. That some do is undeniable. That other Spirit-filled believers do not is equally true. The teaching that tongues *must* accompany the baptism of the Spirit is a divisive doctrine which often leads to a subtle spiritual pride for some and frustration for others.

The Epistles of the New Testament were written to explain and interpret the historical events recorded in the Gospels and Acts, providing the doctrinal basis of our faith. The Epistles have much to say about the fullness of the Holy Spirit in the life of the believer, but nowhere do the Epistles teach that tongues must accompany this fullness. What took place at Pentecost (Acts 2), in the household of Cornelius (Acts 10), and among the Ephesians (Acts 19) are historical events with a given purpose at that particular time. That such events must necessarily be duplicated in the experience of every believer is nowhere taught in Scripture, while the Bible does clearly teach that every believer should be filled with the Spirit who indwells him.

In all the Epistles, from Romans to Jude, speaking in tongues is referred to only in I Corinthians 12-14. If this gift or sign were necessary for every believer, it is odd that the New Testament puts such little stress on it. It is likewise odd that the only church where Paul dealt with this matter in writing was the Church of Corinth. Here was every kind of sin and vice: divisions, contentions, carnal practices, fornication which could scarcely be mentioned for its perversion, criticism of leaders, marital tangles, brother going to law against brother, profaning of the Lord's table, etc. Hardly a picture of Spirit-filled believers! By contrast we have no evidence that the Philippian church, for example, where love and joy were the dominant notes, ever experienced tongues in their midst. Were they not filled with the Spirit? All nine *fruits* of the Spirit (Gal. 5:22, 23) are to be manifested in the life of every believer, but nowhere do we find that all the *gifts* (or even any specific gift) must be demonstrated by every believer. If this were true, the teaching of the "Body of Christ," with its many members exercising different functions, each dependent on the other, would lose its significance. Each gift contributes to the edification of others, but not all members are expected to exercise every gift.

Any attempt to induce the outward manifestations of the gifts of the Spirit (e.g., the use of unknown phrases to start the flow of speaking in tongues) is a fleshly effort which can result in grave errors. The Holy Spirit does not need our human interventions in order to bestow upon us His gifts. What He desires is a humble and contrite heart which is submitted in complete surrender to Himself.

4. The exercise of the gifts of the Spirit must be done "decently and in order" (I Cor. 14:40), for "God is not the author of confusion, but of peace" (I Cor. 14:33). Where disorderliness results, there has either been a counterfeiting work of Satan or a misunderstanding of the true manifestations of the Holy Spirit.

IV. Exaltation of the Person of Christ that men may turn to Him and grow in Him is the primary aim of the ministry of the Word of God.

The history of Christianity is replete with the sad stories of heretical movements within the church which have lost their Scriptural bearings by failing to focus constantly on the Person of Christ. The Bible is Christocentric. Christ is the Author and Finisher of our faith, and we look to Him as such. Christ says of the Comforter, "When he, the Spirit of truth, is come ... he shall glorify me" (John 16:13, 14). It is the work of the Spirit to glorify Christ and not Himself. Therefore, any emphasis on the Spirit of God which tends to minimize or exclude the Person of Christ is an incorrect interpretation of the Scriptures.

Failure to focus properly on Christ not only leads to errors of understanding the work of the Spirit; it also can result in a misunderstanding of Satan and his work. One extreme is to neglect Satan, for all practical purposes, and proceed as if he did not really exist. This allows for the Devil to operate unnoticed. Another extreme is to overemphasize the Devil and his works, attributing far too much to him and his emissaries. This turns our attention from Christ to the enemy of Christ. Paul warns, "Now the Spirit speaketh expressly, that in the latter times some shall depart from the faith, giving heed to seducing spirits, and doctrines of devils" (I Tim. 4:1). We do well to heed that warning today.

Great care should be taken not to attribute to Satan or his demons sins which are really the result of the lust of the individual. There is grave danger in attributing to demons activities which the Word of God specifically calls "the works of the flesh" (Gal. 5:19-21). Any excusing of sin or attempt to deal with sin by exorcising of demons, instead of dealing with the sin itself (such as lust, hatred, jealousy, etc.) in the life of the believer, is avoiding the true issue. Such an approach tends to minimize sin and the responsibility of the individual. "Every man is tempted, when he is drawn away of his own lust, and enticed" (Jas. 1:14).

conclusion

Keeping in mind the guidelines delineated above, the Latin America Mission in Colombia purposes to continue in the work to which God has called us as long as God Himself so indicates. . . .

To this end it is our earnest prayer that God will make us faithful to Himself (including His Son and His Spirit), to His Word, which will always be our guide, and to His people, to whom He has called us.